TOM
OSBORNE
ON
LEADERSHIP

TOM OSBORNE ON LEADERSHIP

Life Lessons from a Three-Time
National Championship Coach

PAT WILLIAMS
with MIKE BABCOCK

Advantage®

Published by Advantage, Charleston, South Carolina.
Member of Advantage Media Group.

ADVANTAGE is a registered trademark and the Advantage colophon is a trademark of Advantage Media Group, Inc.

Printed in the United States of America.

ISBN: 978-159932-379-4
LCCN: 2012955054

This publication is designed to provide accurate and authoritative information in regard to the subject matter covered. It is sold with the understanding that the publisher is not engaged in rendering legal, accounting, or other professional services. If legal advice or other expert assistance is required, the services of a competent professional person should be sought.

Advantage Media Group is proud to be a part of the Tree Neutral™ program. Tree Neutral offsets the number of trees consumed in the production and printing of this book by taking proactive steps such as planting trees in direct proportion to the number of trees used to print books. To learn more about Tree Neutral, please visit **www.treeneutral.com**. To learn more about Advantage's commitment to being a responsible steward of the environment, please visit **www.advantagefamily.com/green**

Advantage Media Group is a leading publisher of business, motivation, and self-help authors. Do you have a manuscript or book idea that you would like to have considered for publication? Please visit **www.amgbook.com** or call **1.866.775.1696**

I dedicate this book to Tommy Ford, Rob Wilson and Mike Babcock, my three researchers and writers on this leadership book series.

‒ PAT WILLIAMS

I dedicate this book to the TeamMates program, established by Tom and Nancy Osborne, as well as to my parents Bab and Dorothy, who loved children — and not just their own.

‒ MIKE BABCOCK

CONTENTS

SEVEN SIDES OF LEADERSHIP

Leadership has become a gigantic industry unto itself in our country. Hardly a week goes by that I don't get another brochure or mailing piece about a leadership conference or seminar or retreat. And that doesn't take into account the books that are pouring out on leadership, seemingly by the day.

I think it all started in 1992 when a man named Donald T. Phillips wrote a book called *Lincoln on Leadership*. He spent years trying to get it published and the publishers told him that the problem was that there's just no place to put it in the bookstores; there's just no category on "leadership." So he was turned down many times.

Finally the book was published and it became a huge success, and an industry was launched in the publishing world. Then, a pastor on the West Coast, John Maxwell, wrote a book called *The 21 Irrefutable Laws of Leadership*. It hit *The New York Times* bestseller list and the barn door was open at that point. Now, leadership books are coming out in droves.

And, many of them are built around people – many of the biblical personalities have been written about. We have David on leadership and Jesus on leadership and Moses on leadership, including one book called *Moses on Management*. And then there are the Civil War personalities – you can read about Robert E. Lee on leadership and Ulysses S.

Grant on leadership, and when you get to World War II, the books are abounding – from Truman on leadership to Eisenhower on leadership to Roosevelt, to Churchill, to General Patton, to General Marshall. It just never ends.

And you can't be in the sports business unless you've written your book on leadership. We have Pat Summitt on leadership and Mike Krzyzewski on leadership and Joe Torre on leadership and Lou Holtz on leadership. But I wanted to hear a few words from Bear Bryant on leadership. I wished that Coach Bryant had written in depth on the topic, but he passed away in 1983. I felt certain that Bryant had a message and advice for leaders both today and in the future.

So I set about writing a book, with the help of Alabama expert Tommy Ford, that might convey the principles and practices of the great Paul "Bear" Bryant. It was an eye-opening experience. The book *Bear Bryant on Leadership* was a commercial success, but even more than that, I think we were able to assemble a fantastic resource from the accounts of the players who played for him, the coaches who coached both for and against him, and the many others whose lives he touched.

The next great in the sports world I wanted to hear from was Bobby Bowden. The result was *Bobby Bowden on Leadership*, written with Rob Wilson, whose involvement with Florida State athletics began as an undergraduate student there in 1982-83.

Next up was Tom Osborne, a logical step when considering college football coaches, though Osborne's leadership has gone beyond the fields of athletic competition. As with the first two books in this on-going project, I am so proud of this project in conjunction with Advantage Media Group. Also, as with the others, the research has been in-depth, with assistance from the Nebraska Athletic Department and my writing partner, Mike Babcock. We've contacted many people who have known Osborne as a coach, politician and now athletic director, a position from which he will soon step aside. Through my interviews, we have brought into clear focus all of Coach Osborne's leadership principles.

I am a fanatic on the subject of leadership. I have bought most of the leadership books over the years; as a matter of fact, I have almost 800 leadership books perched in my leadership library at home. In addition to that, I have spent 54 years at the highest level of college and professional athletics, the last 44 as an executive in the National Basketball Association.

Through all of my study, I came away convinced that to be a leader for the ages, the leader who makes an enormous impact, there are seven qualities or sides of leadership that must be in place. With all due apologies to my good friend John Maxwell and his *21 Irrefutable Laws of Leadership*, this book is designed to focus on these seven sides of leadership that I have discovered all great leaders possess, and match it up with what Coach Osborne has done for over 50 years as a leader. The more I studied Osborne as a leader, and the more interviews I conducted, the more convinced I became that he truly was a seven-sided leader.

Those seven sides are: character, competence, boldness, vision, people skills, serving heart, and communication. That this book includes seven chapters is not coincidental. The focus of each is one of those seven sides, in the order they are listed. However, there are elements of each of the seven sides in each chapter because, ultimately, they are all part of a leadership whole.

As you read the reflections and the teaching points that come from all of these people who know Osborne well, the mission of this book is to make you a better leader, with Osborne as the model. Whether you're leading in education, the military, the church, athletics, business, or the highest levels of government, this book is designed to help you discover the keys to being a seven-sided leader through the life of a college football legend and Hall of Famer, Tom Osborne.

And if you happen to be a college football fan besides, you'll learn a little about the Cornhuskers Osborne coached. That's not the purpose, just a side benefit, resulting from my research.

In any case, sit down and get ready for a read that could change your life. Make sure to take notes, and I hope you end up circling and writing all over this book. Let me conclude the way I concluded this section in the Bryant and Bowden books. I drove by a church once and the marquee read: "The person whose Bible is tattered usually has a life that's not."

Have a productive read!

INTRODUCTION

"I would have had no respect from the players if
we had done anything but what we did."

—TOM OSBORNE
Following the 1984 Orange Bowl game

Nebraska won 255 games during Tom Osborne's 25 seasons as head football coach. The Cornhuskers were national champions three times in the final four of those seasons, and Osborne's final five teams had a combined record of 60-3. Because of such numbers, the College Football Foundation and Hall of Fame waived its three-year waiting period for induction. A year after Osborne stepped aside at age 60, he joined his immediate predecessor at Nebraska, Bob Devaney, in the Hall.

At least nine victories every season, an .836 winning percentage, 13 conference titles and 25 consecutive bowl games help define Osborne. That's the nature of coaching. His first book was titled *More Than Winning*. The title was appropriate to the man. But someone who doesn't win can't write such a book because, again, victories – results – not principles define coaching success.

Osborne's teams lost only 49 times, with three ties. And one of those losses, the 25th, says as much about the man as the victories, the bowl games and the championships. The loss cost Osborne what would have been his first national championship, in just his 11th season. And, as curious as it might sound, he almost certainly would have gotten that championship had he been willing to settle for a tie. The loss came against Miami in the Orange Bowl game, 31-30, on the night of Jan. 2, 1984. Actually, the decision that led to the loss came just after midnight. But first, some context.

The 1983 Huskers were nicknamed the "Scoring Explosion," a nickname given prior to the season, printed on an official schedule poster that featured quarterback Turner Gill, wingback Irving Fryar, and All-America I-back Mike Rozier, already the second-leading rusher in school history. The propriety of the nickname was immediately apparent as Nebraska opened with a 44-6 victory against Penn State in the first Kickoff Classic at Giants Stadium in East Rutherford, New Jersey. The Huskers followed with 56 points against Wyoming and then 84 at Minnesota. Theirs was a video-game attack.

Nebraska led the nation in rushing as well as scoring in 1983, with averages of 402 yards and 52 points per game. The Huskers set NCAA single-season records for touchdowns rushing and passing, total touch-downs, points and extra points by kicking. They also set an NCAA record for "most points scored in a brief period of time," putting up 48 in 9 minutes, 10 seconds of the third quarter against Iowa State. They led 14-12 at halftime and 62-19 by quarter's end. The final score was 72-29.

Osborne's Huskers, whose only close calls were at Oklahoma State (14-10) and rival Oklahoma (28-21), were ranked No. 1 in both major polls from the pre-season to the end of the regular season. As Big Eight champions, they would be Orange Bowl hosts, matched against Miami, ranked No. 5 in the Associated Press poll and No. 4 in the United Press International coaches' poll. Coach Howard Schnellenberger's Hurri-canes had lost only to Florida in the season-opener.

By the time Nebraska traveled to Miami, Rozier, who was only the second collegian to rush for 2,000 yards in a season (Marcus Allen was the first in 1981), had been named the Heisman Trophy winner, and offensive guard Dean Steinkuhler had won the Outland Trophy and Lombardi Award. *Washington Post* columnist Ken Denlinger wrote that Steinkuhler, not Rozier, should have won the Heisman as well. Both had earned All-America honors, Rozier unanimously – along with Fryar.

The high-powered Huskers were double-digit favorites even though Miami was playing on its home field. Schnellenberger did what he could to enhance that advantage, massing support from South Florida, as well as from some Orange Bowl officials, who openly rooted for the Hurricanes on the sideline during the game. He also made the event a spectacle, arriving at media day at the stadium in a helicopter. And through the news media, he encouraged those without tickets to come to the Orange Bowl stadium for the celebration – if the game were close in the fourth quarter, he said.

Miami jumped to a 17-0 lead. Nebraska tied the score at 17 early in the third quarter, only to fall behind 31-17. With 6:55 remaining in the game, the Huskers cut the deficit to 31-24, the score when they took over for the final time with 1:47 remaining. Five plays later, they faced fourth-and-8 at the Miami 24-yard line, with Rozier sidelined by an ankle injury, suffered early in the third quarter. Back-up I-back Jeff Smith, who had scored the previous touchdown, got the ball and carried it into the end zone with 48 seconds on the clock, setting up the drama that would help define his then-46-year-old head coach.

Midway through the season, *Sports Illustrated* proclaimed Nebraska "the greatest team in college football history." Prior to the game, the consensus of opinion was Nebraska's dominance during the regular season was such that the Huskers might be voted national champions even if the Orange Bowl were to end in a tie. And considering how his players had come back from large deficits twice during the game, Osborne might well have been justified in settling for a tie, especially with no timeouts remaining.

Nebraska didn't have time to consider a play for a two-point conversion. And the percentages favored an extra-point kick, of course. Osborne typically played the percentages, which said that the Huskers had no more than a 40-percent chance of a two-point conversion attempt (the rule had been in effect in the college game since 1958) succeeding. Punter Scott Livingston had become the No. 1 placekicker at mid-season and was 38-of-40 on extra-point kicks, including three-for-three that night. Had the responsibility been his, the score almost certainly would have been tied.

The Huskers' long-snapper, Scott Raridon, said afterward he knew he wouldn't be moving from offensive tackle to snap for Livingston at that point. "We'll never tie a game here," he said. "At least I don't think we'll ever tie a game here on purpose."

Ironically, at the coaches' final news conference the previous day, Osborne said as much when asked, hypothetically, if the game came down to kicking a field goal for a tie or trying to win, what he would do. He might call for a field goal if the alternative were a desperation "Hail Mary" pass, he said. "But if it came down to a two-pointer or if it were inside their 10-yard line, I'd have to go for it. I hope the situation doesn't arise because if it does, I'm going to be crucified, one way or the other."

The situation did arise, and Osborne acted as he said he would, a consistency of character to which those who know him will attest in this book. He called a play the Huskers had practiced all season, a pass from Gill to Smith, the junior back-up. And it nearly worked.

But Miami's Ken Calhoun deflected the ball slightly, enough so that it glanced off Smith's shoulder pads, incomplete.

Osborne wasn't crucified for the decision to play for the victory, quite the contrary. He had the support of his players and assistants, to a man. Or if he didn't, no one would step up and admit it. Steinkuhler told reporters he would have felt the same if the game had ended in a tie. That seemed to summarize the feeling in the Husker locker room: You play to win.

The same was true of Husker fans. An estimated 2,000 were at the Lincoln airport to greet and applaud the team on its return from Miami. Even the national press praised Osborne. Milton Richman of the United Press International wrote: "The Nebraska Cornhuskers lost the game but not their dignity. For that they can thank their coach, Tom Osborne. No other coach I can immediately think of embodied good coaching principles more or served as a better model of correctitude to his players." Bill Lyon of Knight-Ridder Newspapers wrote: "In defeat, Nebraska gained humanity." George Vecsey of *The New York Times* wrote: "Osborne showed that he and his team and his college and his state loved winning so much that they would take the chance of losing."

Nebraska's chances of being voted No. 1 with a tie were enhanced by No. 7 Georgia's upset of No. 2 Texas in the Cotton Bowl earlier in the day, an outcome of which Osborne was aware. The Longhorns were the only other undefeated team during the regular season. Because of their loss, Miami climbed to No. 1. Nebraska still received 4½ first-place votes in the final AP poll and 6 in the UPI poll to finish ahead of Auburn, which remained No. 3 after squeezing past Michigan in the Sugar Bowl.

That Osborne's Orange Bowl decision was more studied than spur of the moment, his consistency of purpose in other words, was further reflected a season earlier. The 1982 Big Eight championship would be determined, as it almost always was, by the outcome of the Nebraska-Oklahoma game. Both teams had unblemished conference records but the one-loss Huskers had the higher ranking, No. 3, to two-loss Oklahoma's No. 11. As a result, Orange Bowl officials announced beforehand that should the game end in a tie, the Huskers would get the bid.

On Osborne's weekly radio show, "Talk to Tom," a caller from Lexington, Nebraska, asked whether the Huskers would play for a tie late in the Oklahoma game, under circumstances almost identical to those just over a year later in the Orange Bowl against Miami. He'd go for the win, Osborne said without hesitation, because it would mean a clear-cut conference title.

Osborne's pre-Orange Bowl comment about his being crucified regardless of his decision was reasonable enough, given the expectations of Husker fans. Looked at now, his Hall of Fame career might seem like a steady climb to the national championships in 1994, 1995 and 1997. But it was hardly that. Following Devaney was difficult, and there were times "people wanted to get rid of me; 9-3 wasn't good enough, didn't measure up," Osborne said recently. "So once you've been to the top, then that's the only standard."

Devaney had taken Nebraska to the top, following 6-4 seasons in 1967 and 1968 that led to enough disaffection that a petition for his removal was circulated. The petition followed Devaney's unwillingness to fire assistants. Devaney was loyal to those loyal to him. And Osborne mirrored that trait, so important to effective leadership. In any case, Devaney, weathered the storm, leading the Huskers to national titles in 1970 and 1971, with an offense restructured by Osborne, his offensive ends coach.

Osborne had come to Nebraska in 1962, looking for a coaching position after three seasons in the NFL, the first on the San Francisco

49ers' taxi squad, the last two as a wide receiver for the hapless Washington Redskins. Devaney had just been hired to replace Bill Jennings, who was fired after five losing seasons. In fact, Nebraska had managed only three winning seasons since Biff Jones coached the 1940 team to the school's first bowl game, the Rose Bowl against Stanford.

All three of the winning seasons had come under Bill Glassford (1949-55), who recruited Osborne out of Hastings, Nebraska, High School. Actually, Glassford didn't so much recruit Osborne as simply offer him scholarship aid. Husker basketball coach Jerry Bush also offered scholarship aid to the multi-sport athlete. But Osborne declined, as he did similar offers from Wyoming (football) and Denver University (basketball), deciding to pay his own way to Hastings College.

Osborne attended elementary school in St. Paul, Nebraska. After his father, Charles, returned from military service, the family moved to Hastings, into a house across the street from the Hastings College campus. Osborne's paternal grandfather, also Tom, played football at Hastings College, as did Charles and Tom's own son Mike, a three-year starter at quarterback for the Broncos.

Osborne competed in basketball, track and field, as well as football at Hastings College, as he had at Hastings High. *The Omaha World-Herald* named him its "Nebraska Athlete of the Year" as a high school senior. He played quarterback and safety on the football team, was a 6-foot-3 guard on the basketball team and competed in the 440 and discus for the track and field team. He also ran the hurdles until a muscle tear forced him to back off of that event. In addition, he played for the Hastings American Legion baseball team in the summers; he was the third baseman on a state championship team.

The World-Herald named him the "State College Athlete of the Year" in 1959, after the *Lincoln Journal and Star* conferred the same honor on him in 1958. He was the first Nebraska athlete to win the award in both high school and college.

San Francisco drafted Osborne as a quarterback; he was the 222nd player selected in the 12-team NFL draft. But he moved to receiver in training camp because the 49ers were going to keep only two quarterbacks and they already had Y.A. Tittle and John Brodie.

Football wasn't Osborne's only career choice. He graduated magna cum laude and applied for a Rhodes Scholarship his senior year at Hastings College. Though he wasn't selected for that, he did receive a Rockefeller grant for a year's study in a theological seminary. His paternal grandfather had been a Presbyterian minister. Osborne decided to attend a Presbyterian seminary in San Anselmo, California, because of its proximity to the 49ers' practice facility in Redwood City, California. Even so, the commute was too taxing. Plus, "I realized I missed football too much," said Osborne.

Though on the taxi squad, Osborne made road trips, rooming with Jack Kemp, a young quarterback with limited NFL experience. The two were offered contracts by the Los Angeles Chargers of the fledgling American Football League a year later. Kemp accepted. But Osborne was determined to play in the NFL. When the 49ers released him at the end of training camp in 1960, Washington signed him, probably based on his play against them during an exhibition game, he has said.

Osborne played in all but two games over two seasons with the Redskins and could have continued his NFL career. But a pulled hamstring suffered in training camp in 1961 coupled with issues related to how Washington handled player contracts led to Osborne's decision to move on. He had taken graduate classes at Southern California during the off-season and supervised players in a football dorm there for coach John McKay. He also had considered law school, before deciding to return to Nebraska to continue his graduate studies in educational psychology, with academic administration as his goal.

Since he wasn't ready to give up football just yet, Osborne asked Devaney about being a graduate assistant. He never intended to make coaching a career choice, however. It would just be a way of easing out of athletics. Devaney said the grad-assistant positions were filled but that Osborne could have room and board in exchange for monitoring a group of athletes, mostly football players, who called themselves the "uglies." They were all from out of state, and "we started off being rowdies," Larry Kramer recalled many years later. "You never called Devaney. You told Tom." Kramer, who earned unanimous All-America honors as a tackle in 1964, has credited Osborne with keeping him in school.

The athletes lived in a corner of Selleck Quadrangle, and initially Osborne roomed in that area of the dorm with them. The assignment showed his people skills. "The dorm counselors wouldn't go down there," Osborne said. "The dorm counselors were afraid of them."

Kramer, who went on to a successful coaching career, is among those interviewed for this book about Osborne's leadership. "He was a very consistent and very fair man with all of his players," said Kramer. "The best way to describe Tom is that he's a good man."

Osborne completed a master's degree in educational psychology in 1963 and a Ph.D in 1965, after which he divided his time between coaching football and teaching educational psychology with the academic rank of instructor in the Teachers College. In 1967, at Devaney's insistence, he had to choose between the two. That's when he became a full-time assistant coach.

In 1969, with the back-to-back 6-4 seasons still wearing on him, Devaney told Osborne he was thinking of retiring from coaching in the not-too-distant future and that he wanted Osborne to succeed him.

Devaney was the athletic director, remember. "It really surprised me," said Osborne.

However, as with everything he did, Osborne had a plan. For one thing, he wanted to be a head coach by age 35. For another, he preferred to be a head coach at a school other than Nebraska. Following Devaney would be difficult. After all, despite the 6-4 seasons and the fact that the back-to-back national titles were still to come, Devaney had turned the program around.

Osborne had applied for coaching jobs at South Dakota and Augustana, which offered a still-appealing opportunity to teach as well as coach, and he interviewed at Texas Tech at the end of the 1969 season. Had the Red Raiders' job been offered, he almost certainly would have accepted.

Devaney announced he would step aside following the 1971 season and Osborne would replace him. After the Huskers won a second consecutive national championship, however, Devaney was persuaded to coach another season as Nebraska attempted to win an unprecedented third national title. So Osborne's promotion was delayed until after the 1973 Orange Bowl game. He was 35. He would be just 36 when the Huskers defeated UCLA at Memorial Stadium to open the 1973 season.

Twenty-five years later, Osborne stepped aside, for reasons that included faith, family, health and a concern that if he waited, the program would lose staff continuity. Though Bill Byrne was the athletic director, Osborne was instrumental in choosing his successor, assistant Frank Solich, whom he had promoted to assistant head coach in 1991, preparing for the eventual transition. Solich faced a task similar to the one with which Osborne had dealt in following Devaney. Three national titles in the previous four years was even more pressure. "I knew when I left here, if I had stayed another five or six years, we wouldn't have another five years like we'd had because the mathematics just weren't there," Osborne said recently. "The stars just got aligned with players and chemistry and everything in such a way that we'd have been good. We'd have won a lot of games. But I felt bad because Frank was walking into the same thing that I did when Bob left."

Even though Osborne could have continued to coach, he had made commitments. And when he made commitments, he kept them, despite the personal consequences. Friend Bobby Bowden was still coaching, as was Joe Paterno, and both were older. "The first three or four years I was out of coaching were really hard," said Osborne. "It was really difficult. It was hard for me to even go to a game. I remember Bo Schembechler wrote a book after he retired. Somebody asked him what he would do the first game out. He said he would be in his basement, by himself, with the door locked and the game on TV. And I remember reading that, and I thought 'that's the way I feel' because to go in the stadium on game day and not have any ability to do anything about the outcome, that was really hard when you'd done it for a long time."

Three years out of coaching, Osborne ran for Congress, the House of Representatives seat in Nebraska's Third District, which includes his hometown of Hastings. He received 82 percent of the vote in 2000, 93 percent in 2002 when he ran for re-election, and 87 percent when he was elected to a third term in 2004. In 2005, he announced he would seek the Republican nomination for governor rather than a fourth term in the House. He finished second in the primary to incumbent Dave Heineman, though he received just over 44 percent of the vote.

In mid-October of 2007, with Husker football sliding, Chancellor Harvey Perlman persuaded Osborne to step in as interim athletic director. Two months later, the "interim" designation was dropped. Osborne agreed to remain until at least July of 2010. That date came and passed.

Osborne is still the athletic director as this book is being written. But he will step aside on January 1, 2013. He will remain at the university until August 1, 2013, however, and help his successor, Shawn Eichorst, in the transition. During the news conference at which he was introduced, Eichorst offered an assessment of Osborne that fits the purpose of this book. "I think Warren Buffett said it best about Coach Osborne in Coach's recent book, *Beyond the Final Score*. He said, 'When most people think of Tom Osborne, they think of a great football coach. When I think of Tom Osborne, I think of a man of character who quietly but effectively improves the lives of everyone he encounters."

Throughout his career, in politics as well as in coaching, Osborne has acted on clearly defined principles. As those in this book will attest, Osborne has and does embody the seven sides of leadership: vision, communication, people skills, character, competence, boldness and serving heart. His decision to go for two and victory in the 1984 Orange Bowl game reflected all of those qualities. As the UPI's Richman wrote, he served as a "model of correctitude to his players."

The Huskers "were so confident of their ability to move the ball that to their dying day, they would have felt we could have made the two points," Osborne said. "A lot of players couldn't have lived with it the rest of their lives. I couldn't myself."

Even though those remarks were made nearly 30 years ago, they still characterize his leadership, as you will see in the pages that follow.

Chapter One:

CHARACTER: PERFORMANCE EARNS TRUST

"Adversity doesn't build character, it reveals it."
—TOM OSBORNE

The game wouldn't be at the top of the list if one were to rank the most memorable victories during Tom Osborne's 25 seasons as head coach. Those in bowl games that clinched national championships would, understandably, be first. The 1995 Orange Bowl game against Miami, no doubt, would be No. 1, giving Osborne the first of his three titles. But the 17-14 victory against Oklahoma on November 11, 1978 would have to be in the discussion, at least by those who understand the tenuous nature of coaching and how a bounce of the football can change the course of a coach's career.

The bounce, in this case, was a fumble by Oklahoma running back Billy Sims, the ninth of the game by the Sooners and the sixth lost. Sims gained 17 yards on the play, to give him 153 in the game and increase his season's total to a nation-leading 1,550. Less than a month later, the junior from Hooks, Texas, would be named the Heisman

Trophy winner. Nebraska safety Jeff Hansen, a fifth-year senior who had started for only the third time in his career, was credited with stripping the ball, which senior monster Jim Pillen recovered at the Cornhusker 3-yard line with 3 minutes, 27 seconds remaining.

Oklahoma never got the ball back. Afterward, Pillen told reporters: "When I saw that 1:16 left on the clock and no more timeouts for Oklahoma, I could start to feel that sand sifting through my toes." The victory ensured the Huskers at least a share of the Big Eight championship and a trip to the Orange Bowl. Nebraska hadn't gone to Miami for the holidays since Bob Devaney's final season, when it won a third consecutive Orange Bowl – after two that had produced national championships.

In the celebration that followed the victory, the goal posts were pulled down, something that hadn't happened at Memorial Stadium, as near as anyone could remember anyway, since Halloween of 1959, when Nebraska snapped Oklahoma's 74-game conference unbeaten streak. As long as no one was hurt, Devaney – the athletic director in 1978 – said, he guessed Nebraska could afford new goals posts every 20 or so years. Atop the front page of *Lincoln's Sunday Journal and Star* was: "We did it!" And just below that exclamation, by the weather capsule, was "Frozen joy."

Temperatures that day had been in the 30s, with wind gusting to 25 miles per hour.

Oklahoma had come to Lincoln undefeated, untied and ranked No. 1. Just three years before, the Sooners had won the second of back-to-back national championships. And they appeared poised to win a third for coach Barry Switzer. In fact, in his 1990 autobiography (with Bud Shrake) *Bootlegger's Boy*, Switzer wrote: "I know I have said the 1974 team was the best I ever had at Oklahoma, but on further reflection, the 1978 bunch might have been the best . . . I don't know how

I would compare them, but I do know the 1978 team could have won the national championship as easy as not."

Switzer had been promoted to head coach in 1973, succeeding Chuck Fairbanks, who left to try his hand in the NFL with the New England Patriots. After six seasons, Fairbanks returned to the collegiate ranks, replacing Bill Mallory at Colorado. More about that later. It's a small part of this story.

Osborne also succeeded Devaney as head coach in 1973, of course, and because Nebraska and Oklahoma had been conference rivals since the 1920s, the two were constantly compared. And Switzer's immediate success, the national championships in 1974 and 1975, represented significant adversity for Osborne. Prior to the 1978 game, Osborne was quoted: "The obsession with Oklahoma is getting to me. It's getting pretty hard around here for fans to appreciate a good year without beating Oklahoma."

Osborne's teams were a combined 55-14-2 with two shared Big Eight titles to that point. They had won at least nine games and played in bowls every season. But they were 0-5 against Switzer's Sooners. Counting a loss to Oklahoma in Devaney's final season, Nebraska was 0-6 and hadn't scored so much as a point in the fourth quarter against the Sooners since the "Game of the Century" on Thanksgiving Day of 1971 at Norman.

To make matters worse, only one of Osborne's five losses against Oklahoma had been closer than a two-touchdown deficit. In 1975, the Huskers had taken an unblemished record and No. 2 national ranking to Norman and lost 35-10. After the 1977 game at Norman, a 38-7 loss, Osborne recounted how afterward his oldest daughter, 10-year-old Annie, had vowed, in tears, to move to Oklahoma. His attempt was levity. But the pressure to win against Oklahoma was no laughing matter.

Nebraska had climbed to No. 4 before the Oklahoma game in 1978, with eight consecutive victories following a nationally televised, opening-game loss against Alabama in Birmingham. The Crimson Tide was ranked No. 1 in the Associated Press pre-season poll (the United Press International didn't conduct a pre-season coaches' poll) but would lose two weeks later to Southern California and be ranked No. 3 when Oklahoma went to Lincoln. Undefeated and untied, Penn State was No. 2.

As a result of their upset of Oklahoma, the Huskers moved past Alabama to No. 2, behind Penn State. If Nebraska could win a final regular-season game at home against unranked Missouri and Penn State could beat rival Pittsburgh a week later, the Huskers would play the Nittany Lions in the Orange Bowl with a national championship at stake. As an independent, Penn State could choose its bowl game. And it would almost certainly choose the bowl that offered the highest-ranked opponent.

Penn State defeated Pittsburgh. But Nebraska lost to Missouri, coached by former Husker assistant Warren Powers, ending Nebraska's national championship opportunity. And to make matters worse, Orange Bowl officials decided to invite Oklahoma for a rematch with Nebraska. Osborne could savor his first victory against Switzer's Sooners for only a week. How's that for dealing with adversity?

In the aftermath of the regular season, before bowl preparations began in earnest, Osborne interviewed for the Colorado job. Buffaloes Athletic Director Eddie Crowder contacted him after firing Mallory. Osborne, like Devaney, didn't make such decisions based only on self-interest. "We talked about it as a staff," he recalled years later. "And the staff thought we ought to at least look at it. We were getting some heat here . . . couldn't beat Oklahoma."

Osborne was serious in his consideration of the job. "I wasn't bluffing," he said later. "I really thought I would take the job when I went out there."

Colorado offered triple the salary and less pressure. Plus, the state was a fisherman's paradise. And for Osborne, fishing wasn't too, too far behind faith and family. The process went far enough that he and wife Nancy flew to Boulder, Colorado, and he addressed the team. As he talked with the Buffalo players, however, he realized he couldn't coach them against the players he had recruited to Nebraska. He just wouldn't feel right about that, he said afterward.

Devaney also had opportunities to leave Nebraska. "I know he had a chance at one point to go to Indiana as head coach," Osborne once recalled. "And I remember sitting in a room; he had the whole staff there, and he wanted to know if they were in favor of going or not. So many coaches would have decided what was best for them, if it was more money for them, just take off and leave their staff, maybe take one or two guys. But it was a package deal. You guys want to go or you want to stay?

"I think the vote was to stay. So that's what we did. He was very loyal. He didn't really want to go forward without the people around him."

Though Osborne was talking about Devaney, he could have been talking about himself. That's character. That's people skills. That's a serving heart. That's communication. That's leadership.

As noted elsewhere in this book, Osborne's Hall of Fame career was not a steady rise to the national championships finish. He endured criticism and stayed the course – by staying at Nebraska, a decision applauded by most Husker fans but one that didn't alleviate the pressure. He dealt with plenty of adversity after that, much of it related to Oklahoma until Switzer left Norman following the 1988 season.

Nebraska lost the Orange Bowl rematch with Oklahoma at the end of the 1978 season and didn't defeat the Sooners again until the 1981 season, when Mike Rozier joined Turner Gill and Irving Fryar in what would become "The Scoring Explosion" backfield in 1983, as recounted earlier in this book.

Switzer, who had aggressively recruited Gill out of high school in Fort Worth, Texas, would lead the Sooners to another national championship in 1985, giving him three, and compile a 157-29-4 record (.837) in his 16 seasons. Osborne's record during those same 16 seasons was 158-36-2 (.811). But he was only 5-12 in games against Switzer. And the manner in which Nebraska lost some of those 12 times gave rise to the term "Sooner Magic."

In 1976, the Huskers led 17-13 when Oklahoma quarterback Thomas Lott handed the ball to Woodie Shepard and the halfback passed to Steve Rhodes, a play that covered 47 yards and carried to the Nebraska 35 yard line with 3:30 remaining. Then on third-down-and-19, Dean Blevins, also a quarterback, passed to Rhodes, who lateraled to running back Elvis Peacock for a 32-yard gain to the Huskers' 2-yard line. Those were Oklahoma's only passes of the game. Peacock scored the winning touchdown on the next play, with 38 seconds remaining.

In 1986, Oklahoma drove 94 yards on 11 plays to tie the score at 17 with 1:22 remaining. The drive was kept alive by a facemask penalty that nullified a lost Sooner fumble – they had already lost two fumbles in the fourth quarter – with 4:10 on the clock. The tying touchdown came on a 17-yard pass from quarterback Jamelle Holieway to tight end Keith Jackson. Oklahoma got the ball back, after forcing a punt, at its own 35-yard line with 50 seconds on the clock. Four plays later, on third-and-12 from the Sooners' 45-yard line, Holieway and Jackson teamed on a 41-yard pass play. Tim Lashar kicked a 31-yard field goal with 6 seconds remaining for the victory.

That was among the more frustrating losses during his career, Osborne said in a 1998 interview because had the facemask penalty not been called the Huskers "had the game won."

A year later, in a Big Eight scheduling adjustment, Oklahoma returned to Nebraska and won a game billed as the "Game of the Century II." Though the 17-7 final score didn't reflect it, the Sooners dominated. But that's beside the point here. Oklahoma and Nebraska had been No. 1 and No. 2 in the national rankings from the pre-season on. Yet the week of their showdown, voters inexplicably reversed the order, even though the Huskers had the previous Saturday off while Oklahoma defeated Missouri. Though they probably didn't need extra motivation, the Sooners were given it.

There was no "Sooner Magic," of course. But it wasn't all about coaching, either. Proximity to Texas, rich in high school talent, gave Switzer a recruiting advantage. After Switzer moved on to the NFL's Dallas Cowboys, Nebraska dominated Oklahoma. Osborne's record against the post-Switzer Sooners was 8-1. His final three teams outscored Oklahoma by a combined 179-28.

That Osborne persevered despite the adversity of fan frustration with Oklahoma reflects his character, as did his decision to remain at Nebraska when Colorado came calling. The Oklahoma frustration also showed another aspect of his ability as a leader. He could adapt and did throughout his coaching career. As the chapter on vision shows, Osborne was always forward thinking, a step ahead, capable of seeing the big picture and then acting accordingly, fostering confidence in those he led.

Ironically, Oklahoma contributed significantly to Nebraska's success overall because the Sooners were the model for the offense that came to define the Huskers under Osborne. He was Devaney's receivers coach, remember, and his early teams as head coach were pass-oriented. That changed dramatically, however, in large part because of "Sooner Magic."

"We went through a series of difficult experiences with Oklahoma," Osborne said in a 1998 interview. "The first five or six years I was head coach we had two or three instances where we had them on the ropes, had a pretty good shot at them, and they had a quarterback who would scramble on third down, run an option, make a big play, and quite often, it had to do with athleticism and bail them out, third-and-15 or something and the guy would either scramble and hit a pass or scramble and run for a first down. So I think it was along about 1979, 1980, that I became convinced the best way to win college football games, particularly if you had to beat Oklahoma, was to have someone with athleticism and speed at quarterback. So we began to look at speed as a basic prerequisite of the whole deal."

The quarterbacks on his early teams were pro-style, pocket passers, including Dave Humm and Vince Ferragamo, both of whom earned All-America honors in his system. "Probably the first guy I recruited who was as much of a runner as he was a passer was Jeff Quinn," said Osborne. Those who followed included Gill, Steve Taylor and Tommie Frazier, as well as Scott Frost, who transferred to Nebraska after two seasons at Stanford following a high school career in Wood River, Nebraska.

"That was, I guess, the first major shift that I can remember in coaching philosophy. I think at one point we were recruiting quarterbacks primarily for their throwing ability, and then we began to recruit quarterbacks . . . we wanted them to be good throwers, if possible, but we wanted them above all to be good athletes and good runners."

There was more to his commitment to a run-oriented offense than just using Oklahoma as a model. Running quarterbacks were only part of the equation. "I felt in this part of the country, with this kind of weather, that we were going to have to be able, on two or three occasions during the year, to run the ball because the weather conditions were not going to be very good for throwing it. And I knew from experience people weren't going to spot you two or three games a year," Osborne said.

Such thinking illustrated his vision.

Even though Osborne and Switzer had dramatically different personalities, they talked regularly, though not necessarily often. And despite the frustrations with Oklahoma, Husker fans for the most part respected Switzer. In 1980, before the teams played in Lincoln to see which would represent the Big Eight in the Orange Bowl, he made a surprise appearance on the set of Devaney's Friday night show on a local television station and presented Nebraska's athletic director with a bag of tacos.

The tacos were symbolic of the Sun Bowl, where the Huskers would be headed if they lost the next afternoon's game, while the Sooners would go to the Orange Bowl. That was Switzer. It was all in good fun. And that's what happened. Nebraska went to El Paso for the holidays.

"Tom led with character at all times," Switzer said. "The manner in which he carried himself commanded the total respect of his peers. There are many ways to lead, and Tom did it in a silent way. He was extremely intelligent and always carried himself in a classy manner."

At the news conference to announce he was retiring as coach 17 years later, Osborne was asked if he felt like the last of an era of coaches such as Switzer, who was finishing his fourth and final season as coach of the Dallas Cowboys, and Devaney, who had died in May of that year. "I haven't really thought about it," said Osborne. "I miss some of those guys. I miss Barry. It's been a lot of fun."

The victory against Oklahoma in 1978 was certainly a lot of fun for Osborne and the Huskers who played in the game, including Pillen, a senior from tiny Monroe, Nebraska. Pillen was a member of Osborne's second recruiting class, from Lakeview High School in Columbus, located about 20 miles from Monroe. As so many small-town Nebraska boys, Pillen grew up a Husker fan. He regularly listened to legendary radio broadcaster Lyell Bremser describe Nebraska games and attended his first at Memorial Stadium when he was in the fourth grade.

Pillen followed his older brother to Nebraska. Clete Pillen walked on and played linebacker (1974-76), leading the Huskers in tackles his final two seasons. He was a captain as a senior.

Jim Pillen was offered a scholarship and told, depending on his speed, he would play cornerback or safety on defense or I-back, wingback, or even fullback, on offense. During two-a-day practices in the pre-season, the freshmen began about 45 minutes after the varsity.

One day, Osborne jogged past the freshmen, stopped and came back to where Pillen was stretching. Years later, Pillen recalled their brief discussion: "He said, 'I see they've got you at cornerback on the depth chart, Jim. I think you'd be a better monster. Go tell Coach (Guy) Ingles you should be a monster.'

"I was a monster after that," Pillen said. "That was astonishing. That was Tom Osborne. He knew."

Pillen was a very good monster (strong safety), earning first-team All-Big Eight recognition twice. He also was a two-time, first-team Academic All-Big Eight selection as well as an Academic All-American as a senior in 1978. Osborne's walk "was always consistent and disciplined," said Pillen, founder and CEO of Progressive Swine Technologies. "He led by his actions and didn't use a lot of words. His philosophy of leadership was (to) keep it simple and be consistent with your actions.

"Coach Osborne still speaks to me years after my years at Nebraska. The prime message is: 'No matter the circumstances, do your best every day. There's no such thing as a day off. You never stay the same. You're either getting better or getting worse. It's your responsibility to decide what you're going to do.' Because of that philosophy, we felt we could play with any opponent and beat any opponent."

Again, the 1978 Oklahoma game was no better example. Pillen was named the Big Eight Defensive Player of the Week for his performance, which included eight tackles and two fumble recoveries. Defensive end George Andrews and linebackers Lee Kunz and Bruce Dunning also played key roles in containing Oklahoma's high-powered, run-oriented Wishbone offense.

Andrews was a member of Pillen's recruiting class, another Nebraskan, from Omaha. He was a three-year starter, and like Pillen, an excellent student as well, a two-time, first-team Academic All-Big Eight honoree and Academic All-American in 1978. In fact, Andrews played his final season as a graduate student, after the NCAA changed its rules to allow it. He also was a co-captain.

"Coach had a consistency of character that built respect and trust with all of his people," Andrews said. "I like to call it good old-fashioned Midwest character. As a result, people wanted to follow him. Tom was a very disciplined man, who grew as a leader over the years. A long-term successful leader must have a consistency of character or people will see through you and spot you as a phony."

Andrews was a first-round draft pick of the Los Angeles Rams, the 19th player selected, and played six seasons with them. Kunz also played in the NFL, three seasons with the Chicago Bears.

"Tom was very quiet and disciplined as a leader and not the stereotyped head football coach," said Kunz. "He was very trustworthy and had confidence in his players, but not inspiring through his talks. He inspires people to follow him through his actions. Tom worked harder than everyone else, was a student of the game and could pick apart defenses and teach that to his players very well.

"Coach created loyalty with his coaches so that they all stayed together as a unit for years. One of their tenets was to have the older players teach the younger ones, and it worked well. Tom had a moral compass. He didn't preach to us, but we could see what his values were through his example."

Kunz was recruited out of Golden, Colorado. He didn't redshirt, as most did, and started his final two seasons, setting what was at the time a school single-season record for tackles as a junior and leading the team in tackles again as a senior, when he earned second-team All-Big Eight recognition. He also was the conference discus champion in 1978.

Kunz, who has built a successful development company based in Wheat Ridge, Colorado, actively supported Osborne's political career. "As a Congressman, Tom was so demanding of himself," said Kunz. "He was one of the hardest workers out there."

Paul Meyers, an associate athletic director at Nebraska, played baseball for the Huskers, earning All-America recognition from *The Sporting News* as a senior in 1986.

"I think what makes Tom a great leader is his incredible humility," Meyers said. "It is real and very sincere. I think it is difficult to second-guess a leader who lives what he preaches. He also endears himself to his employees because he is so willing to look at himself critically.

"Those who have this level of humility also tend to be great listeners, which Tom is. Finally, I think it is also important to allow your eagles to soar. In other words, let people who are capable of doing a great job do their job. Tom allows us all to do our jobs without a high level of scrutiny."

Meyers oversees the Huskers Athletic Fund.

"In this world of CEO compensation escalation it is normal to get as much as you can get in compensation," said Meyers. "The athletic director prior to Tom Osborne had a total compensation package of close to $600,000 annually. This was merely $250,000 to $300,000 more than his boss, the Chancellor of the University of Nebraska. Tom Osborne, upon accepting the job at Nebraska, made sure that he was not to be paid more than the chancellor. He felt it was important that his boss made more money than he did. It showed Tom's true character."

For the record, Osborne's successor, Shawn Eichorst, will make $973,000 annually, with a five-year contract and a $750,000 bonus if he remains for the life of the contract.

Senior Associate Athletic Director for Academics Dennis LeBlanc has worked in the Nebraska athletic department since 1983 and directed the department's academic program since 1993. He has "studied Tom as a leader very closely," LeBlanc said. "He lets everybody in the department know that whatever their position, they have a very important job to do. If they'll do that job to the best of their ability, great things will happen and everyone will be part of it.

"Tom might say, 'I'm the athletic director, but I'm just a part of all this.' That's how he makes us all feel. In my case, I have a job and Tom has given me the authority to carry it out. But I'm no more important than the custodian who cleans up our offices. With all of Tom's multitude of accomplishments, in his mind, it's no big deal."

Associate Director of Athletic Medicine Jerry Weber joined Nebraska's athletic medicine staff in 1977, Osborne's fifth year as head coach. He has been the head athletic trainer since 1996 and was inducted into the National Athletic Trainers (NATA) Hall of Fame in June of 2011.

"Tom's leadership was marked by his consistency," said Weber. "If you asked him about something on Monday and again on Friday, you'd get the same answer. That's because his character led his thoughts and actions. He was a man of his word and backed it up by how he lived. Tom was always ready for anything that might come up because of his thorough preparation.

"Nothing ever caught him by surprise."

Comments such as those from LeBlanc and Weber might seem to stray from the focus of this chapter, character, but ultimately all aspects of leadership discussed in this book are part of a whole. They could add up to character or vision or boldness or any of the seven principles.

"To be an effective leader, you must have your life priorities and principles in order," Husker head coach Bo Pelini said. "It starts there. You can't compromise your standards if you don't have them. Tom Osborne won't ever compromise his principles because that's what leadership is all about. And he's always surrounded himself with people who share his views about life and leadership."

Pelini is a case in point. Though his coaching style is markedly different from what Osborne's was, Pelini's principles are much the same, including family, faith and loyalty. And like Osborne, he emphasizes academics, a reflection of his own experiences as a safety at Ohio State.

Pelini started two seasons, earned four letters and was a captain his senior year. He also was a three-time Academic All-Big Ten honoree.

Osborne "set the standard for academic achievement and was the architect of the weight training, nutrition, academic support system and Total Person program that is the envy of his peers," said Jim Rose, a former radio voice of the Huskers as well as a Husker historian. "In his 35 years on campus, Nebraska football was never cited for a major NCAA violation and only had one official letter of inquiry, regarding player vehicle registrations in 1985, and the NCAA eventually took no action, yet to me, his greatest moment as the leader of the program came at one of the lowest points of his career."

That point is described in the introductory chapter on Osborne, the 1984 Orange Bowl game.

Rose offers insight into Osborne's "keen ability to identify a player's strengths and gifts" from the 1995 national championship season, something which might fit better in another chapter. But again, it's all part of a whole that can be identified in multiple ways.

"Nebraska is winning handily at Missouri," Rose said. "In the third quarter, Coach Osborne inserts freshman offensive lineman Aaron Taylor into the lineup. On Taylor's first series he is beaten badly by making technical mistakes. The result is a loss of yardage, and the Huskers are forced to punt.

"Coming off the field, Tom grabs Taylor and chews him out. 'I put you in there for a reason and that is to do your job, not to do everybody else's job, just yours. If I didn't think you could do it, you'd never have made the field.' Taylor went on to become a first-team All-American (twice) and won the Outland Trophy in 1997 as the nation's premier lineman."

Osborne has always been characterized by consistency. "From the beginning of his career, Tom has preached process, process, process," said Rose. "Essentially, the outcome is very secondary to the process. Control what you can control and don't worry about that which you cannot control. You can control preparation. You can control decision-making. You can control your game plan. The players came to know little else about their head coach, and they followed him."

Rose recounts another story to illustrate his point.

In 1986, "the NCAA launched a program to crack down on the loose operation universities had for the 'pass gates.' This is the gate at the stadium where friends and families of players could get into the game," he said. "There was loose patrolling of the gates across college football, inviting illegal activity. Then NCAA President Walter Byers declared 60 Nebraska football players ineligible for the season-opener against Florida State one week before the game.

"All of it was over a question as to whether the Nebraska players were getting too many passes to either give to non-family members or sell for profit. Coach Osborne was faced with the prospect of starting third- and fourth-string players at every position if the decision wasn't enjoined.

"Behind the scenes, he and Athletic Director Bob Devaney and the university lawyers worked to resolve the situation, but in front of the team, he was calm, focused, and his message was very consistent, to ensure the players bought into 'the system.' It worked. No interruption in preparations, and when the NCAA relented and lifted the suspensions, Nebraska dominated the game."

The pre-season No. 8-ranked Huskers defeated No. 11 Florida State 34-17.

Jeff Quinn is mentioned earlier in this chapter, the first quarterback recruited by Osborne who was as much a runner as a passer. Quinn came from Ord, Nebraska, and earned the starting job as a junior, though a leg injury in the opening game sidelined him until the final three games of the season.

Quinn earned second-team All-Big Eight recognition as a senior and finished as Nebraska's career-rushing leader among quarterbacks. He also was a two-time Academic All-Big Eight honoree.

"When I think of Tom as a leader, I think of the word 'integrity,'" said Quinn. "I think of his calmness under fire. I never remember him getting mad. Coach loved the game and the coaches and players he worked with. His belief in God was the centerpiece of his life, and that, along with his love of his family, helped his whole life come together. Coach is the finest person I've ever been around.

"He's a great man and one we all look up to. I wish I could be half the man he is."

Osborne recruited Bobby Newcombe 20 years later. Newcombe, who was born in Sierra Leone, was a quarterback and the New Mexico player of the year at Highland High School in Albuquerque. He began his Husker career as a wide receiver, however, playing as a true freshman on the 1997 national championship team, in Osborne's last season as head coach.

Newcombe was the definitive Osborne recruit. He started six games, despite being hampered by a knee injury as a sophomore, and the first two as a junior, before moving to wide receiver for the good of the team – Eric Crouch, who would earn the Heisman Trophy in 2001, became the starting quarterback. Newcombe also excelled as a punt returner. His game-breaking ability drew comparisons to Johnny Rodgers, the Huskers' first Heisman Trophy winner in 1972.

Newcombe's 94-yard punt return against Missouri in 2000 was a school record, and he finished his career second on Nebraska's all-time list for punt-return yardage.

Definitive Osborne recruit? Newcombe finished a business management degree in three years.

"There are not a lot of men out there like Tom Osborne, who are so genuine and committed to their life values," Newcombe said. "Coach was consistent with his character and modeled what he believed. He walked it and talked it every day. No one is perfect, but Coach was a true example to all of us. That's the reason people from all over seemed to gravitate to him. I admire and respect Coach Osborne. I only played one season under him, but he's always been available to me to this day."

Osborne has always been available to everyone who played for him, as many point out in this book, including Rodgers, for whom Osborne was position coach. "He encouraged me before I left to come back and finish (a degree)," Rodgers said in an interview after he received a degree. "He has always encouraged me to do it, but I don't think he thought I would carry through."

Osborne stuck with Rodgers through off-the-field issues and has said of the Husker nicknamed "The Jet," he "could impact a football game in more ways than anyone I've been involved with."

Rodgers was a sophomore on Nebraska's first national championship team in 1970 and junior on the second in 1971. "As great as that team was, take Johnny Rodgers out of there on kickoff and punt returns and it probably wouldn't have gone 13-0," Osborne has said.

"He did an awful lot for the kicking game."

Likewise, Osborne did an awful lot for Rodgers. "Tom had the ability to apply discipline and put it into action," said Rodgers. "He was very focused on discipline and conditioning. Tom Osborne's ability to focus was: follow one course until (you) succeed."

Yes, the first letter of each word spells "focus."

"Coach stressed to us that whoever gets tired first is going to get beat," Rodgers said.

Getting beat wasn't something that happened often during Osborne's 36 years as assistant and head coach. "At Nebraska, winning isn't everything," said Rodgers. "But it's right up there with oxygen."

Jim Walden said of Rodgers' ability as a kick returner, quoted by the Associated Press in 1992: "Once you've been around a Johnny Rodgers, it's all kind of downhill after that in my lifetime."

Walden was a full-time Husker assistant in 1971 and 1972, when Rodgers won the Heisman Trophy, after two seasons as a graduate assistant under Devaney, who had coached him as a player at Wyoming, on teams that won two Western Athletic Conference championships.

Walden later was the head coach at Washington State (1978-86) and Iowa State (1987-94). His Cyclones defeated Nebraska 19-10 at Ames, Iowa in 1992, one of just four victories that season. It was the only time in 25 seasons that an Osborne-coached team lost to an opponent that finished with a losing record.

"Tom was totally dedicated to the job he had to do at Nebraska," Walden said of Osborne. "The kids knew they'd be thoroughly prepared for what was ahead. That gave them a lot of confidence as they went into every game."

Patrick Tyrance, the Huskers' first football scholarship recruit out of Millard (Nebraska) North High School, was a two-time first-team all-conference linebacker and a first-team Academic All-American as a senior in 1990, after earning second-team honors the previous year.

"Coach has always been a very principled leader, with a strong set of values," said Tyrance, an orthopedic surgeon. "Those values allow him to make difficult decisions, which may be unpopular but are always based on sound reasoning. Coach led by example. He lived his leadership philosophy right in front of us. If you can see it, it sure is a lot easier to be an enthusiastic follower. Coach Osborne was great at putting the benefits and interests of others in front of his own."

Tyrance was a Husker co-captain in 1990, as was offensive guard Jim Wanek, also a scholarship recruit from Aurora, Nebraska, where he was a state shot put champion as well as an all-state lineman. Wanek was a two-year starter and two-time Academic All-Big Eight selection.

Osborne "was a man of great integrity," Wanek said. "Tom always walked the talk. He stressed to his players faith, family and academics, in that order. Tom lived his life that way and wanted that for his players. Coach wanted all of us to get our degrees and be contributing members of society."

Milt Tenopir was Wanek's position coach, along with Dan Young. Osborne always had two full-time assistants working with the offensive line. Tenopir joined the staff in 1974, replacing Bill Myles, and stayed through Osborne's retirement and five seasons beyond, under Frank Solich.

Tenopir first worked with Clete Fischer, who was succeeded by Young in 1986. Tenopir contributed significantly to Nebraska's rich offensive line tradition.

Staff stability, as will be discussed later in this book, was among many factors in Osborne's coaching success. "Tom had nine assistants and we all had our egos," said Tenopir. "He was able to mold those egos and get us moving in one direction. Tom let us do our jobs and didn't micro-manage like a lot of head coaches. He trusted us and let us coach. I think that's why we had such longevity on the Nebraska staff. We couldn't have had a better boss."

Jack Pierce was a Husker assistant for 13 years and served as the off-campus recruiting coordinator for the last five of those years. He is now a fund-raiser in the athletic department.

Osborne "believed in people and as a result, everyone bought into his leadership approach," Pierce said. "He exudes confidence in people, and that's a big deal in football and life. It drove people to do their best for him. When I first joined Tom's staff (in 1979), he was a silent leader. But as time went on, he adapted and evolved. He had to move forward because of the type of kids he was recruiting. He was never a yeller and screamer, but he became more of a communicator."

Barry Alvarez, who played linebacker for the Huskers under Devaney (1965-67) and also was a graduate assistant at Nebraska, is the athletic director at Wisconsin, after 16 years as the Badgers' head coach. His teams were a combined 118-73-4, including 8-3 in bowl games.

"Tom is very consistent in all areas of his life," said Alvarez. "What you see with him he lives out every day. He's very intelligent and never has to raise his voice to get a point across. You know what you'll get with Tom better than any coach I've ever known.

"I sit in Big Ten meetings with him. He listens carefully and always offers good viewpoints and opinions from his long years of experience. I'll tell you this, everyone listens to him. He's a special guy."

Tom Ash was the Husker football beat writer for the *Omaha World-Herald* early in Osborne's career as head coach and served as editor *of Huskers Illustrated* after that.

Osborne's "greatest strength as a leader was his personal character," Ash said. "It was impeccable. He was able to impart that to others without shoving it down their throats. Many leaders don't know how to transfer their values to others without being overbearing about it. Tom never brow-beat people. He just lives his life. People notice that. Tom leads by example, and that sums up who the man is.

"Tom had personal qualities far above the norm. He had a great ability to transfer those qualities to his team without forcing it on them. There is no one I hold in higher regard."

George Achola, like George Andrews who was quoted earlier in this chapter, played his final season (1991) under Osborne as a graduate student. Achola was a scholarship recruit out of Creighton Prep High School in Omaha, a back-up I-back at Nebraska, not because he lacked talent but rather because of those ahead of him. Osborne's Huskers always had depth at I-back.

"Coach was a man of integrity," said Achola. "His approach was always: 'Do as I do not as I say.' He was a man of compassion. He was able to differentiate between the acts of a person and the person himself. I got in trouble one time, and Coach disciplined me, as he should have. The next day it was all over. He treated me as a human being. 'How you doing?' I've never forgotten that experience."

Osborne's compassion and care for his players, and by extension his character, is illustrated in the stories of Anthony Steels and Ricky Simmons, whose Husker careers overlapped.

Steels was a walk-on from Zaragoza, Spain, where he finished high school while his father was assigned to the U.S. Air Force base there. He was a two-year starter at wingback, and three-year letterman, playing 411 minutes as a junior, the most on the team. He also returned kicks.

Oh yes, and he could sing. In fact, he sang the national anthem before his final home game at Nebraska in 1981, then went out and caught a touchdown pass in a 31-7 victory against Iowa State.

Steels signed as a free agent and played briefly during two seasons in the NFL with the San Diego Chargers and Buffalo Bills. He became addicted to cocaine and spent time in prison. "One of the biggest reasons I never gave up on myself is because Coach Osborne never gave up on me," Steels told Huskers.com. "He's been well aware of my struggles and provided great support."

Steels is now a licensed alcohol and drug abuse counselor.

"Coach had high moral and spiritual principles, and he led us by those principles," said Steels. "He never compromised his character or the principles he lived by. Coach taught us by the way he lived his life. When I played at Nebraska, I knew Coach Osborne was a special person, but I couldn't wrap my brain around all he was teaching us about life. However, as years went by, I understood why the deep life-lessons he was teaching back then had such importance to me as an adult."

Simmons' experience has mirrored that of Steels in many ways, though he came to Nebraska from Greenville, Texas, as a scholarship recruit, not a walk-on, along with high school teammate Nate Mason.

Simmons began as a wingback. He was a back-up at the position as a sophomore in 1980, behind Steels, then moved to split end during a redshirt season in 1981. His only career touchdown pass reception was a 61-yarder against New Mexico State in 1982, the longest of the season. And he was the Huskers' second-leading receiver as a senior, with 13 catches for 137 yards. Osborne's teams were heavily run-oriented by then, remember, so Simmons had to block in order to play.

He had a strong family background. His dad was a principal; his mom taught remedial reading in an elementary school. But Simmons developed a cocaine addiction during a brief career in the short-lived United States Football League. And that addiction led to three stints in prison.

During the third, at the state prison in Tecumseh, Nebraska, Simmons received a letter from Osborne in 2008. In the letter, Osborne said he knew that Simmons' parents had believed in him and that he, Osborne, believed in him also. So when he was released from prison in December of 2009, Osborne offered to do whatever he could to help his former player.

"The fact he took time out of his day to even acknowledge me . . . I can never repay him for that," Simmons told Steven M. Sipple of the *Lincoln (Nebraska) Journal Star*. "When I received Coach Osborne's letter, it just told me, 'You know what, there is still someone out there who cares, who believes in me.'"

Simmons has been sober since his release and is now a licensed alcohol and drug counselor who runs an outpatient program in Lincoln. He also does motivational speaking.

"When I think of Tom Osborne as a leader, here's what I think of: accountability, commitment, dedication, loyalty, a work ethic second to none, 'never give up,'" said Simmons.

"Coach taught me to be a true man and a good person. He taught me to treat people the way you'd like to be treated in return. I have the utmost respect for the man. I go to see him once a week, just to show him I care for him as a person."

And also to show that Osborne's belief in him hasn't been misplaced.

Chapter Two:

COMPETENCE: THE KEY IS PREPARATION

"Trophies and whistles and bells and rings don't excite me that much."
—TOM OSBORNE

As we pointed out in the introductory section on Tom Osborne, disaffected fans circulated a petition calling for the dismissal of coach Bob Devaney following Nebraska's 6-4 records in 1967 and 1968. First, those fans wanted Devaney to get rid of some assistants. When he refused, the petition was drafted. Devaney later joked that he hadn't known about the petition because his secretary shielded him from such things, dumping negative letters in the trash. Had he known about the petition, Devaney said, he probably would have signed it, too.

The disaffection was evidence of how quickly things can turn for a coach. Prior to Devaney's arrival in 1962, back-to-back 6-4 seasons would have been applauded. But he had produced five consecutive seasons of nine or more wins and five bowl appearances, and the standard had changed.

Bowl-game losses against Alabama following the 1965 (Orange) and 1966 (Sugar) seasons influenced a change in philosophy that contributed to the back-to-back 6-4 seasons. The Huskers had tried to play the way Alabama did. "They had had small offensive linemen," Osborne said, recalling those games. "We began to recruit some small offensive linemen, guys that were quick but not very big." As a result, "we were getting pushed around," he said. "We had a little trouble blocking people." A quick fix was needed. As the petition dramatically underscored, the clock was ticking on Devaney and his staff.

The solution to the problem illustrated Devaney's ability to adapt, another element of leadership that Osborne would mirror as politician and athletic director as well as coach. The Huskers' system had been to develop players, and particularly offensive linemen, beginning in the freshman program – remember, under NCAA rules, freshmen weren't eligible for varsity competition until 1972. But "we realized that we maybe weren't given a lot of time to develop a freshman offensive line," said Osborne, "so Bob suggested maybe I go to California, start looking at the junior colleges."

Nebraska hadn't recruited in California before that, not consistently anyway. And only two or three Californians had earned Husker football letters to that point. "The conventional wisdom around here was that a California kid would come in here and quit and go home," Osborne said. "Once they hit the cold weather, they just wouldn't stay."

Bob Newton stayed.

Newton earned junior college All-America honorable-mention recognition at Cerritos (California) College, after a similarly successful career at John Glenn High School in Norwalk, California. He was an offensive tackle, listed at 6-foot-3 and 235 pounds his first year at Nebraska. His nickname was "Big Fig" and he attracted recruiters from several big-time schools, among them Oklahoma, the Huskers' Big Eight rival.

"Big Fig" made an official recruiting visit to Nebraska in December of 1968, as Osborne recalls. "That was back when they didn't have jetways (in Lincoln), obviously, so he landed out here at the old airport, and Bob came strolling off that plane onto the tarmac in a T-shirt," said Osborne. "It was probably 10 or 15 degrees, and he had to walk about a hundred yards to the terminal, and I could see the wheels turning in his mind, that this probably wasn't a very good idea."

Had Newton based his decision on the weather, he wouldn't have become a Husker. He picked Nebraska over the other schools, in large part, because of Osborne. "His humility, sincerity and genuineness during the recruiting process was a major leadership example to me and helped me decide to enroll," Newton said. "His persistence and preservation were also major assets that influenced me to sign with Nebraska. Coach Osborne out-recruited all of them because of those qualities."

That Osborne sold Newton on Nebraska because of personal qualities such as humility, sincerity and genuineness helped keep Newton in Lincoln as well. "Big Fig" stayed for reasons beyond the challenge of getting the Huskers back on track after seasons that were "sub-standard for the University of Nebraska," he said. Even though he was from California, he understood the dynamics of that.

With time of the essence, "the coaching staff implemented a gruesome winter-ball conditioning program, which was to toughen us up as a football team," said Newton. "One of the stations included a 12-minute distance run which Coach Osborne facilitated by running with us. He must have run that drill eight to 12 times during a session and demonstrated great physical conditioning and endurance. I could constantly hear him during the run telling me and other teammates to pick it up regarding our running pace. He had a good sense of when to push you, and this is a quality of great leadership."

A willingness to do what is asked of those being led also is a quality of great leadership, and Osborne was always willing to do that, from staying after practice to throw passes to wingback Johnny Rodgers, Nebraska's first Heisman Trophy winner, to running stadium steps with Isaiah Hipp, an I-back who borrowed money for a plane ticket to get from his home in Chapin, South Carolina, to Lincoln so he could pay his own way as a walk-on to play for the Huskers. Osborne didn't distance himself from those he coached, or taught might be a better description of his relationship with them.

But back to Newton, who became the starter at left tackle his first season at Nebraska. His second, and final season, he took another step, earning consensus All-America honors on the Huskers' first national championship team. That team included several other junior college transfers who played important roles in the offensive line, among them Dick Rupert, who started alongside Newton, at left guard. Rupert came from Harbor Junior College in Los Angeles, the year after Newton, as did guard Keith Wortman from Rio Hondo Junior College in Whittier, California, and tackle Carl Johnson from Phoenix (Arizona) Junior College. Wortman and Johnson also were in the regular rotation in 1970.

In any case, "it was a monumental effort to get him here," Osborne said of Newton, who came to Lincoln to begin classes crammed in a Volkswagen with Bob Terrio, a transfer from Fullerton, California, Junior College. Terrio was recruited as a fullback and sat out his first season at Nebraska, before starting at linebacker on both of Devaney's national championship teams.

"Once you got one or two (from California), it got easier," said Osborne. "But to get the first ones, there wasn't anybody here from

California. Then we began to get quite a few of them." During his 25 seasons as head coach, more than two dozen Californians earned letters, including four All-Americans.

Newton was a third-round pick of the Chicago Bears in the 1971 NFL draft. He played five seasons with the Bears, starting the first four, and then six seasons with the Seattle Seahawks, all as a starter. After being drafted, "I remember seeing Coach Osborne, and he stated to me, 'Be sure you finish your education, Bob, because you can't play football forever.' I basically ignored that suggestion but never forgot it," Newton said. "Coach Osborne always communicated and suggested to his athletes to set spirituality, education and athletics as priorities in life, and in that order."

As another chapter in this book emphasizes, communication is a quality essential to leadership. Communication has many elements. Osborne's running distances with Newton and the others in the off-season conditioning program was an aspect of communication, as was his encouraging Newton to think beyond football and the sincerity to which Newton referred in discussing Osborne's selling him on Nebraska. Osborne's words had meaning. They weren't empty.

Newton will attest to that. He works at the Betty Ford Center in Rancho Mirage, California, as a consultant, after 12 years as a lead counselor, a journey best presented by Newton. In July of 1983, two years after his NFL career was over, he wrote to Osborne.

"I had been admitted into treatment for alcohol-drug rehabilitation and wanted Osborne to know the severity of the problem and that I 'was trying to do something about it,'" said Newton. "Coach Osborne wrote me right back, supporting me, and said I was doing the right thing to help myself. He also wrote in the letter when I got on my feet to come back to the university and he would hire me as a graduate assistant freshman offensive line coach and I could complete my degree. I believe leadership is providing hope to others, and this letter from Osborne gave me some hope and direction while I was feeling pretty hopeless in the treatment center. I have been in recovery for almost 29 years since that treatment experience, and the spark of hope I received from Coach Osborne's letter was a major contributor for me to continue treatment and remain sober."

After he left the treatment center, Newton returned to Nebraska and served as a graduate assistant coach with the freshman team in 1984, while completing a bachelor's degree – at age 35. "It was Coach Osborne's motivation and remarks about the importance of education that fueled my decision to return to school," Newton said. "This motivation continued, and I completed my master's degree at age 55."

Leadership can involve caring about individuals, as Newton explains. When Osborne was serving in the House of Representatives, Newton got a call from his former coach, "asking me if I would appear in front of a Congressional hearing regarding underage drinking. He was chairman for the committee and was very concerned about the affects alcohol use has on young people who are under 21," said Newton. "I was extremely grateful he asked me to participate as an expert witness in trying to reduce underage drinking. For many years, while he was still head coach at Nebraska, he had me speak in front of his teams regarding the dangers of alcohol-drug abuse. I believe his all-around care for the individual athlete and people in general are a major leadership quality."

Keith Zimmer agrees with Newton. Zimmer is an Associate Athletic Director for Life Skills and member of the Nebraska Athletics Executive Team.

"What makes Tom Osborne a good leader? Tom Osborne excels as a leader because he sees the big picture and promotes total-person development," said Zimmer. "As a head coach, he encouraged his players to live a balanced lifestyle, striving for success in academics, athletics and life. The results during his coaching career supported his total-person philosophy as Nebraska had more football Academic All-Americans than any other school."

During Osborne's 25 seasons as head coach, 40 of his players earned first-team Academic All-America honors, including 12 who did it twice. His three national championship teams included seven first-team Academic All-Americans, four of whom earned that recognition twice.

His "philosophy as a coach helped me shape and create our current Life Skills program in Nebraska Athletics, which now serves over 600 student-athletes with a total of five professionals providing services in proactive education, individualized support, career and personal development," said Zimmer. "Tom Osborne leads by example, is always well-prepared and serves with confidence and attentiveness. He is competitive in nature and promotes success at all levels, but as one of his books is titled, it is about *More Than Winning*, and this mantra is what made Dr. Tom Osborne an outstanding leader."

Aaron Graham was among Osborne's 40 Academic All-Americans, earning first-team recognition in 1995, after receiving second-team honors as a junior in 1994. He was a three-time Academic All-Big Eight honoree as well as a Today's Top Eight Award winner as a senior.

Graham's academic success complemented his on-field success. He was a four-year letterman and the starting center on Osborne's national championship teams in 1994 and 1995. In fact, he was the only player in the interior offensive line to start on both teams, earning All-America honors as a senior.

"There are all kinds of coaching methods and ways to develop young male athletes into men," said Graham. "Tom did it through his example. He had earned a Ph.D. in psychology, and he used that to turn us into productive young men. Coach never got super-excited or really depressed.

"The worst profanity he'd ever use was 'dadgummit!' "

Osborne rarely showed his emotions on the sideline. Doing so "may have felt good to the person at the time, but it didn't serve any purpose," he has said. "A lot of times it's for show. The fans see that, they want to see how much he cares. But if you really cared, you'd keep your head in the game. Getting a penalty or not being able to communicate to the players is the worst thing you can do."

Reserved or not, that wasn't a problem for him. "His ability to communicate exactly what he wanted you to do was exceptional and always produced the results he wanted," Graham said. "Coach could say less and get more accomplished through his style than any coach out there."

Texas was a recruiting emphasis for Osborne, and Graham was among those from the Lone Star State who cast their lot with the Huskers, coming from Denton. He redshirted as a freshman then earned a letter primarily as a long-snapper. He started the last four games as a sophomore, stepping in after right guard Brenden Stai suffered a broken leg and Ken Mehlin, who had been the starting center, moved to right guard. Graham held the starting job for the remainder of his career and was elected co-captain as a senior. In 1994, he had to adjust to three different quarterbacks because of injury, yet the offense never missed a beat on the way to giving Osborne his first national championship.

Graham was a fourth-round draft pick of the Arizona Cardinals in 1996 and played six seasons in the NFL, the first four with the Cardinals, for whom he started 40 games.

Nebraska, and Osborne, prepared him for success beyond the playing field. He has made Nebraska his home. He lives in Gretna, Nebraska, and owns Premier Outdoor Properties.

"Every day when we came into our team meeting, Coach never opened up with football issues. He'd talk about life in general, our classwork and other stuff," said Graham. "He'd focus on things that were important to young guys and things we were struggling with. Coach Osborne's rules were cut-and-dried: Be focused on your job and your role on the team."

Stai came to Nebraska from Yorba Linda, California, another area in which Nebraska had recruiting success under Osborne, as discussed at the beginning of this chapter. He earned four letters as an offensive guard but didn't really come into his own until his senior year.

As a sophomore Stai backed up Outland Trophy winner Will Shields. He was the starter in 1993, after Shields moved on to the NFL, but seven games into the season, he suffered the broken leg. Stai also played in the shadow of right tackle Zach Wiegert, a member of the same recruiting class, and a rare three-time, first-team All-Big Eight selection. When they were seniors, Wiegert was a unanimous All-American and won the Outland Trophy.

Stai also earned All-America recognition on Osborne's first national championship team, a consensus pick. It was only the fourth time since 1950 that two offensive linemen from the same team were All-Americans in the same season. He was a third-round draft pick of the Pittsburgh Steelers in 1995 and played eight seasons in the NFL, starting 96 games.

"Coach Osborne has and will always exemplify leadership through his unwavering commitment to those around him," said Stai, who returned to Nebraska, where he is a coaching intern. "Good, bad or otherwise, Coach Osborne consistently gave each and every one on his team, coaches, players, staff and administration, the ability to succeed, whether it was empowering his coaching staff or helping a player get through adversity. Coach Osborne still exudes great leadership."

Former Husker volleyball coach Terry Pettit was on staff with Osborne at Nebraska for 21 of Osborne's 25 seasons as head coach and provides perspective, not only as a coach but also as one who has been involved in leadership training since he left coaching after the 1999 season.

"Tom has always been in synch with the culture of the state of Nebraska," said Pettit. "He has the ideal personality for the people of that state. His competitive drive is strong, and I think the last eight years as head coach he ramped it up even more; he was even more focused."

Those last eight years were the 1990s. Though his teams continued to win at least nine games and play in bowl games every year, Osborne had begun to question whether the game might have passed him by. At least that's what his comments to a handful of Nebraska reporters, following an Orange Bowl luncheon before a game against Miami, following the 1991 season, seemed to indicate.

The Huskers had lost four consecutive bowl games and would lose three more before snapping the streak. Some fans complained that the problem was lack of passing. Osborne was too committed to the run, they said. The problem, however, had more to do with the passing of opponents.

Nebraska's run-oriented offense worked just fine in the Big Eight, a cold-weather conference for the most part, as did its 5-2 base-alignment defense. So the Huskers were regular contenders for conference titles during the 1980s, winning or sharing five and finishing second four times. But their bowl games were in warm-weather cities (or the Sugar Bowl's Superdome) against warm-weather, passing teams, including Miami twice in its home stadium, the Orange Bowl.

Part of the solution, a significant part in fact, was Osborne's decision to change his defense to a 4-3 base alignment, a change he was reluctant to make initially for fear it wouldn't hold up against the run-oriented teams in the Big Eight. The dynamic in the conference was to play as the best teams played, and Nebraska and Oklahoma, consistently the best teams, had option offenses. There were other factors in Nebraska's success in the 1990s, of course. Even so, the change to a 4-3 base defense was a reflection of Osborne's willingness to change as well as the focus to which Pettit referred.

The Huskers' record in those last eight seasons was 87-11-1, with six Big Eight championships, including five outright. And eight of those 11 losses and the tie came in the first three of those eight seasons. Remember, Osborne's record in the final five seasons was 60-3, with three national championships and a wide-left field goal attempt as time ran out away from a fourth.

Numbers don't describe leadership qualities. They can, however, quantify it.

"Tom was able to maintain his complementary people a long time," Pettit said. "He kept that staff together for years. That built up a great deal of trust. In particular, Tom's quarterbacks had a great deal of trust in him. He would never embarrass them publicly."

Staff stability is discussed elsewhere in this book, and quarterbacks are quoted throughout.

Mickey Joseph was among Osborne's quarterbacks in the late 1980s, arguably the most prominent member of the 1987 recruiting class. At the time, Osborne described him as probably the most-publicized quarterback the Huskers had ever recruited.

Joseph was a *USA Today* and *Parade Magazine* prep All-American and the Louisiana offensive player of the year as a senior at Archbishop Shaw High School in suburban New Orleans. Oklahoma considered him the nation's best wishbone quarterback recruit. Joseph's decision came down to Nebraska and the rival Sooners, adding to the publicity surrounding his recruitment.

Joseph redshirted his first season then was a back-up to starter Steve Taylor and Gerry Gdowski, who succeeded Taylor as the starter when Joseph was a sophomore. Joseph succeeded Gdowski in 1990, as a junior, and earned all-conference honorable mention, passing for a Big Eight-best-tying 11 touchdowns and rushing for a team-high 10 touchdowns. But in the final regular-season game at Oklahoma, Joseph suffered a leg laceration when he was knocked out-of-bounds and into a bench on the sideline. The injury required extensive surgery.

Joseph started the opener his senior season, but an off-the-bench performance earned little-used senior Keithen McCant the opportunity to start the second game. McCant took advantage of the opportunity and never relinquished the job. He was named Big Eight Offensive Player of the Year.

"Tom Osborne is very honest and fair," said Joseph, now the head football coach and assistant softball coach at Langston University. "That's what makes him a good leader."

Back to Pettit before moving on to more testimony about Osborne's leadership skills.

Volleyball is the most successful women's sport at Nebraska, on a foundation laid by Pettit. He was the program's second head coach, arriving in 1977, just in its third year of existence. His record was 694-148. The Huskers won 21 conference championships in his 23 seasons and made 19 consecutive appearances in the NCAA Tournament, reaching the quarterfinals 16 times and the semifinals six times.

They were NCAA champions in 1995, the same year as Osborne's second national championship, and they ranked first or second nationally in attendance nine times.

Like Osborne, Pettit emphasized academics as well as athletics. He coached 18 Academic All-Americans as well as 36 AVCA All-Americans, both totals ranking first in the nation.

After stepping aside as coach, Pettit became a mentor to coaches in the Nebraska athletic department before creating Terry Pettit Coaching Enhancement, based in Fort Collins, Colorado. Among his published works are *The Journey to Extraordinary Coaching* and *Talent and the Secret Life of Teams*.

Osborne "really treats people well who have no power – custodians, secretaries," said Pettit. "He has no ego in that sense. So many big-time coaches and executives tend to be peacocks and start to believe it's all about them. Tom never fell into that trap. Tom knew how to win and how to lose. As a result, no one ever wanted to disappoint him."

Tom Shatel is a sports columnist for the *Omaha (Nebraska) World-Herald*. He joined the staff there on Sept. 1, 1991, a week before an opening-game victory against Utah State, and covered Osborne's national championship teams, the second of which in 1995 included the drama surrounding I-back Lawrence Phillips, who was regarded as a serious Heisman Trophy contender until Osborne suspended him for six games following an off-the-field incident. Osborne's decision to allow Phillips to return late in the season sparked considerable controversy.

"To me, leadership is about a lot of things, but leadership is mostly about trust, unbending trust, almost blind trust," Shatel said, echoing what Pettit and others have said. "You would do anything a leader tells you to, walk off a cliff, train in unimaginable heat or play through an injury, because you have that much trust, that much belief, in your leader.

"I've seen it for years with Tom Osborne. People have this incredible trust in Osborne. The best example, for me, remains the Lawrence Phillips incident. There was a huge uproar about whether to play Phillips again. Here in Nebraska it was split, maybe 60-40, maybe 70-30, favoring Phillips coming back. But even those who thought it was a bad idea trusted that Osborne was doing it for the right reasons, that he was trying to help the kid."

Osborne "got destroyed by the national media that year," said Shatel. "But I never read one comment that said he was trying to win at all costs. A lot of columnists and critics said he was misguided, but almost all agreed he was trying to save the kid. That's trust. It's very unusual for sports. I think Dean Smith had that, John Wooden, Coach K (Mike Krzyzewski), a few others. To me, that transcends the playing field. People trusted Osborne to win games and call good plays.

"Off the field there was that trust, too. Now, there's one glaring exception to this. The good folks of Nebraska didn't trust Osborne so much that they wanted him to be their governor. There was no rubber stamp there. Osborne lost the primary. But, I always like to say, the people of Nebraska are smart. They wanted him available to be athletic director, which is a more important job than governor, anyway."

Before the gubernatorial primary in 2005, Osborne went to Washington, D.C., to the House of Representatives. "As a Congressman, I represented a large geographical district. The third district covered 80 percent of the state, mostly small towns," Osborne said. "The people wanted to see me, so I traveled continuously. I was back and forth to Washington every weekend because I cared about the needs of the people in my district. We were flooded with mail and e-mails and needed two full staffs to stay on top of everything. We had eight people in Washington and eight in Nebraska.

"I told them, 'We hired you to do a job, so go do it. Make decisions, go to meetings, do what you think best. You don't have to clear everything with the chief of staff.'"

As was the case with his coaching staff, Osborne didn't micromanage. He delegated responsibility, while paying the same attention to detail that served him so well as a coach.

"I found that leadership in Washington was very partisan," he said. "There didn't seem to be great concern for the greater good. Many people were willing to run for office, but not many would take a stand on their principles. So often the prime concern was simply to be re-elected and therefore it was more expedient to not take a stand or remain silent. And, of course, there was the influence of money, which had many officials obligated."

Such considerations didn't influence the way Osborne went about his business, as Michael Castle notes. Castle is a former governor and former U.S. Representative from Delaware, the state's longest-serving representative, in fact. He met Osborne during his time in Washington. "Being a bit of a sports fanatic, I was well aware of his unparalleled success as the Nebraska football coach," said Castle, now a lawyer in Wilmington, Delaware, after losing the Republican primary for a United States Senate run.

"While I had only observed Coach Osborne when Nebraska football games were on television, he seemed to be very organized in his decision-making ability and very much in control of the Nebraska game situations and his own emotions. Not surprisingly, those distant observations were confirmed when we met and got to know each other. Tom is in every sense of the word a gentleman.

"Relatively – compared to most members of Congress – quiet and soft-spoken, he proved quickly to be thoughtful, an intelligent and informed decision-maker and a real asset to the Republican Party. He would lead by example in speeches or quiet conversations with other members of staff when we were on the floor of the House. He never once, to my knowledge, made a fuss about his great success at the helm of Nebraska football."

Osborne "was equally liked and admired by Republicans and Democrats," Castle said. "His demeanor was such that you could easily imagine how the players he recruited for football and their families became instant Cornhusker devotees."

Bruce Mathison, who came from Superior, Wisconsin, is an example of Castle's point.

Mathison earned two letters at Nebraska but saw little action. His most memorable game was in his senior season, 1982, when he came off the bench late in the first half of a game against Missouri, after starter Turner Gill suffered a concussion and led a 23-19 comeback victory. The Huskers trailed 13-9 in the fourth quarter when he directed an 11-play, 70-yard touchdown drive for the lead with 4:45 remaining and then scored what proved to be the winning touchdown on a 16-yard run just over 2 minutes later, following an interception.

The only touchdown pass of Mathison's collegiate career had come earlier that season, 61 yards to split end Ricky Simmons against New Mexico State.

Osborne's "communication skills are unbelievable," said Mathison. "It doesn't matter who he's talking with, he can relate to anyone. When Tom goes into a home to recruit, he usually closes the deal. When my folks met Coach, they said, 'Bruce, you're going to Nebraska.' "

Despite his limited experience at Nebraska, Mathison's quarter-back skills were such that he spent five seasons in the NFL, including one (1985) in which he played in 10 games with the Buffalo Bills.

In short, "the House of Representatives lost a great Congressman when Tom left," Castle said. "But the University of Nebraska was a winner when Tom returned as athletic director."

Kent Pavelka is a former radio voice of the Huskers. "The three E's: ethics, example, expectation; Tom embodied them all," he said. "If you worked with or played for him, the three E's were a constant. That's what made Tom a great leader."

Herschel Nissensen observed Osborne in his position as the Associated Press College Football Editor from 1969 to 1988. "He had great players and obviously knew how to coach them," said Nissensen. "There was just something about Tom . . . maybe it was because he was a good guy."

Nice guys finish last, according to baseball's Leo Durocher, who was elected to the Hall of Fame in 1994, the year Osborne got the first of his national championships. Durocher was wrong in that instance.

"Tom is a genuine person, who cares about young people and the right causes in life. His value system is in place, and he won't move from it," Bill Snyder said.

Snyder is in his second term as head football coach at Kansas State, and in many ways mirrors Osborne, with whom he competed for nine of his 17 seasons during his first term (1989-2005) in Manhattan, Kansas. He took a moribund Wildcat program and achieved remarkable success. The Kansas State football media guide refers to him as the "architect of the greatest turnaround in the history of college football." And such a designation would seem to be justified.

Going into the 2012 season, Snyder's record at Kansas State was 159-82-1 (.662), including 89-64-1 in conference play. In 1993, he joined Nebraska's Bob Devaney as the only coach in Big Eight history to be named the Associated Press conference coach of the year three times in four seasons. He has been the national coach of the year three times.

"Tom resides in an extremely significant class of quality leaders in this country," said Snyder, who returned to coach the Wildcats in the 2009 season. He also resides in that class. Among other things off the field, he serves as chairman of the Kansas Mentors Council and on the board of directors for the Kansas Leadership Council.

Osborne "was a different type of leader. He was a soft-spoken guy and low-key," former BYU coach Lavell Edwards said. "I visited his practices one spring and there was no question who was in charge. He was unobtrusive to those around him, but totally in control.

"Tom had high expectations for his program and could convey it without being overly demonstrative. He knew what to do and had the ability to instill his vision to his coaches, players, the university, the community and the entire state of Nebraska."

Edwards' assessment carries the weight of a Hall of Fame coach with a career record at BYU of 257-101-3 over 29 seasons (1972-2000). Coaches who have either played for him or worked for him include Mike Holmgren, Steve Sarkisian, Norm Chow, Kyle Whittingham, Brian Billick and Andy Reid.

Osborne "had a great knowledge of the game and could convey it to his players," said Edwards, who directed the Cougars to a national championship in 1984. "He also had the ability to listen well. With Tom, it was never, 'My way or the highway.'"

Big Ten Commissioner Jim Delany worked with Osborne as Nebraska made the transition from the Big 12 to the Big Ten. "I had preconceived notions about Tom's terrific career as an athlete, coach, Congressman and athletic administrator," Delany said. "I also had high expectations about Tom the person. The first thing I noticed . . . when I first met him was the tremendous humility that enveloped him. He's an incredibly humble guy, given all the success he's achieved in every phase of his career.

Osborne "has a big presence, but a humble, understated personality," said Delany. "As an athletic director, Tom listens carefully and is thorough, articulate, mature and patient. He doesn't over-react and jump to conclusions. He has a strong and powerful presence, but his humility gets your attention first. He speaks quietly, but people listen closely to hear what he has to say.

"Tom has great respect for the Big Ten Conference and its culture and wants to contribute where he can. He's willing to support what's best for the overall good of the conference and bring agreement for the best long-term benefit of the group. Tom can disagree, but he's never disagreeable."

The overall good of the group or team and trust have been recurrent themes in this chapter, with an overriding emphasis on competence, a quality that can encompass all aspects of leadership.

Tim Clare has seen those qualities in Osborne. "He developed the trust in those he led. Tom's followers knew that if they'd follow his lead, success would be there for you. You'd accomplish your goals as well as the team's goals," Clare said.

Nebraska football runs in the Clare family. Tim's dad, Pat Clare, was a captain in 1961 and has been a team orthopedist since 1974, Osborne's second season as head coach. Tim Clare was a Husker defensive back for one season before a knee injury ended his career. He's a lawyer in Lincoln now and a member of the University of Nebraska Board of Regents, as well as a member of the three-person board overseeing the construction of the arena in which the Nebraska men's and women's basketball teams will play.

"Tom was a tireless worker," said Clare. "He was a stickler about preparation for anything that could possibly unfold in a game. The lesson was also about being prepared for anything that might take place later in life."

Jim McFarland is passionate in his support of Osborne, his position coach at Nebraska under Bob Devaney. What sets Osborne apart from many leaders "is that he has practiced his Christian faith in all aspects of his life, including his coaching, his marriage, his parenting, his mentoring, his public service," said McFarland, an attorney in Lincoln and former state senator.

"Too many people, including many Nebraskans, take Coach Osborne for granted. He was a great coach. He loves his wife and children. His son and daughters are remarkable young people. He has helped countless people, including football players like me, as well as the people to whom his TeamMates program mentors. People are better persons when they are in his presence. And he was a model public servant, putting the interests of his constituents and the country above party loyalties or partisan politics. How many men have achieved that type of success in all aspects of their life?"

McFarland would fit well in the next chapter, with its focus on walk-ons. He walked on twice, first following graduation from North Platte, Nebraska, High School in 1965, as a quarterback or split end. When that didn't work out, he focused on baseball, the sport for which he was recruited.

After talking with Osborne and showing a willingness to spend a season on the scout team, however, he gave football another try. He was second on the team in receptions in 1968, catching 23 passes for 244 yards and a team-high four touchdowns, and followed with 32 catches for 406 yards in 1969.

Among the more memorable plays his senior season was a pass he didn't catch. The Huskers trailed Kansas 17-14 and faced fourth-down-and-16 at their own 37-yard line with time running out. Quarterback Jerry Tagge, under pressure, threw a desperation pass intended for McFarland.

Though the ball sailed over the 6-foot-4 McFarland's head, Kansas was called for pass interference. Then, another Jayhawk defender drew a personal foul penalty for an obscenity directed at an official, and the Huskers had a first down at the Kansas 17-yard line. Three plays and another personal foul on the Jayhawks later, the ball was at the 6-yard line, from where I-back Jeff Kinney carried it into the end zone with 1:22 remaining. Nebraska's defense held on to the 21-17 victory, which initiated a 32-game unbeaten streak that included national championships in 1970 and 1971.

But back to McFarland and Osborne's leadership. Let McFarland, who went on to play six seasons in the NFL (including five with the St. Louis Cardinals), take it from here.

"The truly extraordinary man is truly the ordinary man," said McFarland. "In addition to Coach Osborne's way of life, I notice many traits that seem fairly ordinary in a societal context but are really extraordinary in a sports context.

"Most athletes and coaches have big egos. They like to display them. Some wear fancy suits or coats. Coach Osborne is always conservatively dressed, modest suits and sport coats, shirts and pants always clean and pressed, conservative yet classy ties, colors always matched and coordinated.

"Some wear expensive jewelry or display their gaudy championship rings. When their photographs are taken, they most always have their Super Bowl or national championship rings prominently displayed in their photographs. I have never seen Coach Osborne wear expensive jewelry or any of his numerous conference or championship rings, or even a bowl watch for that matter.

"As I recall, those awards were mostly located in his downstairs room in his home, which I saw when he hosted a fundraiser there back when he was running for governor. I had to make a special trip downstairs or I never would have known what he did with those awards. The only jewelry that I have seen him wear is his gold wristwatch and his wedding ring. That is one of the few things about him that I have been able to successfully emulate. I wear a Union Pacific retirement watch given to me by my father and my wedding ring. My simple gold-band wedding ring is the only ring I wear."

McFarland continues: "Some have very flamboyant signatures. I have seen both athletes and coaches, and politicians for that matter, practice signing their autographs so their signatures will be distinctive. When Coach Osborne signs his autograph, his signature is traditional Palmer-script handwriting. His signature is often accompanied by an encouraging, handwritten message to the person requesting the autograph.

"Some coaches and athletes drive very expensive cars, Bentleys, Mercedes, BMWs, Cadillacs, or at least a Lexus. When Coach Osborne was the receivers coach in the late 60s, he drove a Nash Rambler station wagon," McFarland said. "Recently, I have seen him driving a Chevy Tahoe SUV."

Adrian Fiala also knew Osborne as a Devaney assistant, though he played on the opposite side of the ball. He was a teammate of McFarland's, in fact. Fiala was a linebacker (1967-69), a Blackshirt, and later a color analyst on the Husker radio network. During that time, he was a regular in the football office, picking up film to study in preparation for the broadcasts. He still does sports talk radio in Lincoln.

Osborne was in charge of the players' study hall when Fiala was a freshman. "I was walking across the campus when I heard someone calling out my name; it was Coach Osborne," Fiala recalled. "He wanted to talk with me about my attendance at the study program. So my first meeting with Coach was not about football. It was about my education."

Fiala has seen Osborne develop as a leader over the years, obviously. But there's also a consistency that's always been there. "Tom has a great aura of confidence, and it comes off to everyone else," said Fiala. "Nothing rattles him, and he doesn't waver in his convictions. His players and staff feel the strength of that; he moves it into his people. Even when Tom is under the gun, he stays calm.

"When you sit down and talk with Tom, you know right away that he knows what he's doing. You feel a lot of trust in him because he has that presence about him. After all these years, the player-coach relationship remains firmly in place."

The relationship with players was what appealed most to Osborne, as his remarks on the day he announced his retirement from coaching – Dec. 10, 1997, four days after the No. 2-ranked Huskers defeated Texas A&M 54-15 in the Big 12 Championship game to earn a bid to play No. 3 Tennessee in the Orange Bowl for what proved to be the coaches' national championship.

"The hardest thing was talking to the players because those are the people I care a great deal about," Osborne said, unable to hold back his emotions. "The thing I enjoy about coaching is the players and the coaches, and I will miss them very much."

Concern for the players and coaches was among the reasons he was stepping aside at that time, he said. Otherwise, "at some point, they may end up with a guy coming in from the outside who treats them differently than they've been treated. All of a sudden, everything they've had that's familiar is taken away from them. So continuity has been critical, as far as I'm concerned.

"What happens to the players and what happens to the staff has been critical. It's been a major part of all my thinking, really, for the last two or three years."

Prior to the news conference, Osborne met with his players. "They were all sitting there, and I tried to think of a couple of things I thought were kind of funny," he said. "Nobody laughed. So I felt really bad. But it was hard because, as I said, I care very much about those guys. That's been the most difficult thing. Hopefully, they'll realize at some point I tried to do what was best for them long-term. I really believe that's what I'm doing right now, to do what's in their best interests."

Keep in mind that Osborne was 60-years-old, at the top of the college football world. He could have continued coaching had the decision been based only on his best interests, not the interests of others.

Earlier in this chapter, Terry Pettit talked about Osborne's increased focus in his final eight years as coach. Prior to the 1992 Orange Bowl, a 22-0 loss against No. 1-ranked Miami, Osborne talked how he felt about never having won a national championship.

"People ask me that quite often," he replied. "I think they expect me to lie and say it doesn't mean anything. I would have liked to have done it, but I would not say that's the over-riding ambition in my life. I feel I have coached a couple of teams that have been good enough to have been national champions. That means more to me."

It was never about trophies and whistles and bells and rings.

Chapter Three:

BOLDNESS: DARE TO DIVERSIFY

"The effort of the walk-ons provides the physical and emotional backbone of the Nebraska program."

—MALCOLM MORAN, *New York Times*, AUG. 1988

itch Krenk was not a heavily recruited football player out of high school in Nebraska City, Nebraska. no 5-star or 4-star or 3-star or even 2-star ranking for him. "I was not a big recruit," he said more than 30 years later, reflecting on a playing career that earned him two Big Eight championship rings and, oh yes, a Super Bowl XX ring. He was on the Chicago Bears' roster in 1985.

The rings are a reflection of Krenk's work ethic and perseverance, to be sure. But they also are a credit to his coach at Nebraska, Tom Osborne. "Coach led young men and gave all of them an equal opportunity and worked with them to become the best players and people they could be," said Krenk, who has his own construction business in Nebraska City. "Coach Osborne gave a kid like me, and lots of others, an opportunity to play and develop, just like all the big-time recruits.

"That was his approach and thus, all the coaches and trainers under him treated every player equally. Something like that has to start at the top. At age 52, I often reflect about how different my life would have been without all the lessons I learned under Coach Osborne."

Krenk graduated from high school in the spring of 1978, with visions of playing football at Nebraska, even though the Cornhuskers showed no interest in him. No major-college recruiters were interested, in fact. Peru State College might have offered financial aid. Krenk doesn't remember for sure. But the NAIA school did show some interest, if for no other reason than it's just 20 miles from Nebraska City.

The University of Nebraska is 50 miles away, and Krenk drove those 50 miles that summer, determined to pay his own way and walk on to the football team. He pulled up to the building housing the coaches' offices, then at the south end of Memorial Stadium, and walked in. He rode the elevator to the second floor and asked a secretary if he could speak to Coach Osborne.

Osborne came out of his office. Krenk introduced himself and said something like: "I was wondering if I could walk on." Looking back, he was naïve, Krenk said, if not a bit presumptuous. Even so, Osborne asked how his grades had been in school. He had earned mostly A's and B's, Krenk assured the coach. Osborne said, OK, if Krenk enrolled for fall-semester classes, he could walk on.

As Krenk remembers, about 150 freshmen reported for the first day of practice, the majority walk-ons. The NCAA had reduced scholarship limits from 45 per year to 30, and Osborne had begun holding back a couple of the allotted 30 scholarships to reward walk-ons who worked their way up on the depth chart to the top two teams. Krenk earned a scholarship at mid-term his junior year. He would have received it at the start of the year had one been available. Osborne apologized for the wait.

Though 150 Husker hopefuls might seem high, Nebraska accommodated such large numbers with a freshman-junior varsity team that had its own coaches and played its own abbreviated schedule. Guy Ingles, a senior split end on Bob Devaney's first national championship team in 1970, was the freshman head coach. Osborne had been his position coach under Devaney.

Ingles asked Krenk his name that first day of freshman practice in 1978 and then asked if he had ever played tight end. Krenk said he had played tight end "a little bit" during his senior season in high school.

Ingles: "How about starting out at tight end?"

Krenk: "I think I'd be a better linebacker, Coach."

Ingles pointed to where the new linebackers were assembling. Besides numerous walk-ons, four scholarship freshmen were listed as possible linebackers. Plus, the scholarship recruiting class included a linebacker who had transferred from junior college. In contrast, the incoming class included only two tight ends, one of which was already slated to sit out as a redshirt.

Krenk: "OK, Coach, I'm a tight end."

By the end of the first week of practice, a third of those freshmen who had reported were gone. Some realized college football wasn't for them. The rest were cut. Krenk, the tight end, remained.

After the season, during the winter conditioning program, more walk-ons were cut. Again, Krenk survived, even though he was a member of the "dirt group," non-recruited walk-ons whose workouts were conducted in what was called the "mushroom gardens," an area below the east stands of Memorial Stadium where the Nebraska track and field team had once competed indoors. The track and the infield area were dirt surfaces, fine dirt, layers of dust, hence the nickname "dirt group."

Krenk and his "dirt-group" associates jumped rope and did up-downs in the dust of the "mushroom-gardens" while the rest of the team, including recruited walk-ons, worked out in the field house, where artificial turf had been installed. Originally its floor had been dirt, as well. Separating the groups was a matter of space. There were simply too many players for the field house.

Osborne's walk-on program offered an opportunity for those who took advantage of it. "Dirt group" or not, Krenk worked hard, pushing himself in conditioning drills. One day, some assistant coaches came to the "mushroom gardens" to watch. Krenk continued to push. At the end of the session, he was asked his name and told to join those in the field house. The rest in the "dirt group" could leave. "Thanks for your time" they were told as they left the "mushroom gardens" and the program.

Though he had survived the "dirt group," Krenk still was a long way from playing. He practiced on the scout team as a redshirt his second year and continued to practice on the scout team his third year, a rare situation for a sophomore. His name hadn't even been included among 128 on the roster in the 1979 media guide, and he was listed fifth on the depth chart at tight end in the 1980 media guide: Jersey No. 89, 6-foot-3, 208 pounds. Krenk would see 14 minutes of game action that season.

Krenk's commitment paid off, however. Though he started only one game at Nebraska, he was a regular for two seasons, alternating with Jamie Williams, a two-time All-Big Eight selection – and the scholarship recruit who had redshirted as a freshman.

By his senior year, Krenk was the strongest tight end in Husker history, with a 375-pound bench press, 100 pounds more than he had been able to lift as a freshman. He had increased his vertical jump to 33½ inches. And he had lost the middle toe on his right foot to cancer.

What was thought to be calcium deposits turned out to be cancerous. The diagnosis was a rare bone cancer, Ewing's sarcoma. The news came early in the spring of 1982 and led to Krenk's traveling to the Mayo Clinic in Rochester, Minnesota, for the operation. Krenk returned to play his senior season.

After finishing at Nebraska, Krenk signed as a free agent with the Seattle Seahawks and survived until the final cuts. Since he hadn't finished a degree at Nebraska, Osborne invited him to return to school and serve as a grad assistant, coaching the tight ends on the Husker freshman team.

Krenk tried the NFL again in 1984, and after being released by the Dallas Cowboys, again near the end of training camp, when the final cuts were made, he signed with the Bears.

Krenk's story is both unique and typical of those who walked on at Nebraska. "Coach had the ability to make everyone feel that they were contributing to the good of the team. He made you feel part of the process, whether you were on the scout team or a Heisman Trophy candidate."

"That was the key to Nebraska's walk-on program," said Dr. Matt Shaw, a Lincoln, Nebraska, anesthesiologist. "Coach showed interest in you in subtle ways, but he made you feel part of the team. That's a unique leadership quality because he could get ordinary players to do extraordinary things at a very high level."

The 6-foot-3 Shaw weighed 180 pounds when he walked on at Nebraska in 1990, aspiring to play tight end. He grew up in Lincoln a Husker fan. He sold soda during games at Memorial Stadium and waited behind the ropes as the players left the field following games, pleading for wristbands, or any piece of gear from the Huskers. He played football and basketball at Lincoln Northeast High School and gorged himself with peanut-butter-and-jelly sandwiches his mom made for him, in hopes of gaining enough weight to play tight end at Nebraska. That the Huskers didn't show much recruiting interest was, in part, a result of his missing most of his senior season because of a back injury.

Shaw earned three letters and played in every game his final two seasons, starting all but three on the 1994 national championship team. By then, he weighed 235 pounds. His commitment could be measured in other ways as well. He ran the 40-yard dash in an electronically timed 5.04 seconds when he arrived. That had dropped to 4.9 seconds by his senior year, and his vertical jump, a measure of explosiveness, had increased by 8½ inches.

The physical improvement Shaw and Krenk made was a significant factor in their success. And Boyd Epley was a significant factor in that improvement. Typically, walk-ons weren't quite big enough or fast enough or strong enough to attract scholarship offers from major colleges. But they were able to develop in Nebraska's cutting-edge strength and conditioning program.

Epley, who created the program from the ground up, was something of a football walk-on himself, you might say. He transferred to Nebraska from an Arizona junior college to compete as a pole vaulter for the Husker track and field team. He was Nebraska's first 15-foot vaulter indoors, in fact. But a back injury his senior year ended his vaulting career

Epley was a dedicated weight lifter, and in the fall of 1969, Osborne asked if he would be willing to supervise Nebraska's weight room. Football players who lifted were more the exception than the rule then, but Osborne sold head coach Bob Devaney on the idea of adding Epley to the staff. In 1970, he became a graduate assistant, and in 1972, he became the first strength coach in the Big Eight.

"Tom is a great leader because he consistently leads by example," said Epley. "He allowed his players and staff to trust him because they knew he'd do the right thing every time. Tom is honest, and when he looks you in the eye, you know you can count on him 100 percent.

"I worked with Tom for 25 years, and he's been there for my whole adult life. Great character is a requirement for outstanding leadership. That's Tom Osborne through and through."

The strength and conditioning program Epley developed became the model for programs across the country, in the professional ranks as well as colleges. Many of those who worked with Epley at Nebraska went on to oversee programs at other schools. The program also is a testament to Osborne's vision.

So Shaw needed more than peanut butter and jelly sandwiches to achieve his dream, which included earning a scholarship. He was rewarded with one as a senior, but only after a freshman on scholarship quit the team. "It wasn't until around the third game of the season," said Shaw.

Prior to the season, an apologetic Osborne had told him he deserved a scholarship, he had earned it as a starter, but the Huskers were at their NCAA limit, Osborne said. Had the freshman not quit, "I would have gone the whole season paying my way," Shaw said. "I didn't mind. I came in knowing I had to earn it. Not being on the 'payroll' just helped me keep focus on what mattered, winning games. I was proud to be a walk-on, but being awarded the scholarship was nice, too."

Scholarship or not, his dream as a 180-pound freshman had been realized. And Osborne was a significant factor. "Coach kept the fire of that dream burning," said Shaw. "And five years later, I was a starter in the Orange Bowl and blocking future NFL players."

Shaw wasn't the only former walk-on who started the 1995 Orange Bowl game against Miami. Joel Wilks, who received a scholarship as a sophomore, was the starter at offensive left guard. He and Shaw were among 14 walk-ons on the Huskers' top two units for the game, in fact.

Wilks' decision to walk on was more difficult than Shaw's because he had a scholarship offer from Northern Illinois. Nebraska promised a scholarship but after two years, following a redshirt season. "I feel so lucky and fortunate to have been able to play for Coach Osborne," said Wilks.

"He is a legend, and other than my parents, I can't think of someone that I respect more than him. He is such a hard worker. I remember how the night before games, when the team would go to a movie to relax, Coach would be sitting in the front row so he could see his notepad. He would still be taking notes and working while we were all having fun. We all respected him as a leader also because he is so smart. We always knew that we would not be out-coached in any game. We would put in new tweaks for teams depending on tendencies that the coaches would see on film. They always worked.

"We would gash teams on running plays that we would make changes to every week. The media would say that we were boring, running the same old plays. But they didn't know all of the changes that Coach Osborne would make every week. It took me two years to understand our playbook."

Wilks' words can be used to support any of the seven leadership principles presented in this book. "Coach Osborne is very honest and has high integrity," Wilks said. "When he says something, you can put it in the bank that he will follow through with it. He is always straight up with you and will stand by his word. The way he lives his life makes people respect him. He is a Christian, a family man and legendary figure in Nebraska. You never see him get flustered or rattled. He is always calm and under control. We never panicked because our leader never did."

The 1995 Orange Bowl game was an example. "We scored two touchdowns in the fourth quarter to come back and beat Miami. Coach was calling plays like we were at a walk-through in practice. He was calm and always thinking ahead to the next play," Wilks said.

He returned to Lincoln for a game and went to a practice the day before. Osborne was at the practice, as he often is. In addition to evaluating the practice, he was "writing a speech and talking to numerous people who kept interrupting him," said Wilks. "He made time, however, to talk with me for about 15 minutes. He made me feel important.

"Coach listens to others' opinions and values what others have to say. He was always open-minded and trusted his assistant coaches to do their jobs. He kept his assistant coaches around for many years because he treated them right and let them do their jobs. He was the best boss to have."

But "boss" doesn't describe Osborne's leadership approach. "Coach is like a father figure," Wilks said. "You never wanted to let him down. I always wanted him to be proud of me, and I wanted to do well for myself but also for him. We wanted to win a championship so bad for him."

And that's what the 1994 team did.

Wilks' father, Jerry, was a Husker under Bob Devaney. Osborne was a graduate assistant at the time, but worked with the receivers; like his son, Jerry Wilks was an offensive lineman. "So my contact with him at that time, as a player, was minimal," said Jerry Wilks, whose career has been in education.

"I would sum up from my perspective as a parent, Husker supporter and long-time educator in Nebraska, his (Osborne's) leadership qualities as honesty, industry, patience, perseverance, loyalty, courage and, perhaps the highest of all, humility. In other words, he had them all. He was truly a role model for all of us who came in contact with him."

That his son spent five years under Osborne and started on Osborne's first national championship team "was truly a father's dream," Jerry Wilks said.

"I can't say enough about Coach Osborne," said Joel Wilks. "I'm so lucky to have played for and gotten to know him as a man. He has helped to make me who I am today. He does things the right way. All of his former players would do anything for him to this day."

Joel Wilks had a dream of playing for Nebraska, just as Shaw did.

In addition to realizing that dream of playing, and getting a scholarship, Shaw distinguished himself in the classroom, earning first-team Academic All-America honors as a senior. He was among 12 Osborne-era first-team Academic All-Americans who walked on, including four who were so honored twice.

Kelly Saalfeld, a walk-on from Lakeview High School in Columbus, Nebraska, earned Academic All-America recognition as a senior in 1979, when he was also a first-team All-Big Eight center and third-team All-American, according to the *Football News*. Saalfeld was a two-year starter, a two-time academic all-conference honoree, and an immediate believer in Osborne's principle-oriented leadership.

"Coach set us straight as freshmen, on our first day of practice," said Saalfeld, who is now a collegiate football official. "He asked all of us a question: 'How many of you think football is No. 1 in your life?' Most of the hands went up. But Coach said, 'No, that's not it.' He asked about family and told the hand-raisers: 'That's not it.' Coach then told us: 'It should be faith, family, school and football, in that order.' With that brief session, Coach Osborne set a course for our lives. I remember that experience like it was yesterday and will never forget it. That was an 'it' moment in my life."

Mike Tranmer, a walk-on from Lyons, Nebraska, echoes Saalfeld. "I spent five years with Coach Osborne, and his leadership was about life, not football," said Tranmer. "Next to my dad, he was the most influential person in my life. Coach was a true role model, and it didn't have a lot to do with football. He was a strong Christian, and he encouraged that but didn't push it.

"He didn't swear. He stressed doing the right thing and treating people the right way. When I became a parent, that's when all of Coach Osborne's teaching points really hit me. I have modeled a lot of my life around what I learned from Coach Osborne during my playing days at Nebraska."

Like many walk-ons, Tranmer was a long shot. He earned all-state recognition in high school but lacked size and speed to play at the major college level. He weighed barely 200 pounds and ran the 40-yard dash in 5.26 seconds as a freshman, when he tried both offensive guard and middle guard on the freshman-junior varsity team. After that first season, Osborne "said to me, 'Mike, I don't think you'll ever play at Nebraska. I'll be happy to help you transfer,'" Tranmer said.

"Coach didn't say that to be mean but to help me. He was totally honest with everyone. I said, 'Coach, I'm staying here and I'm going to show you I can play.'"

Tranmer gained 20 pounds at Nebraska. He dropped his 40-yard dash time to 4.92 seconds and increased his bench press from 310 pounds to 405 pounds; he was named the team's lifter of the year as a senior in 1983. He also started at middle guard and was voted a co-captain by his teammates. He was the definitive walk-on, paying his own way from the beginning of his Husker career to the end.

Ten other co-captains during Osborne's 25 seasons walked on, including Doug Welniak and Jim Scott, who transferred to Nebraska from Kearney State College – now Nebraska-Kearney.

Scott played eight-man football at Ansley, Nebraska, High School, nose guard on defense and center on offense. He sat out a season after transferring then earned a letter as a back-up center, playing in four games in 1990. As a junior, he shared time, starting four games. As a senior, he started every game and earned first-team All-Big Eight recognition, as well as All-America honorable mention from the *Football News*. He also was an Academic All-District VII honoree and a CFA/Hitachi Scholar-Athlete.

In the early 1990s, Osborne changed his system, defensively as well as offensively, and Nebraska's focus became playing for a national championship. "When Tom made a decision, he went with it and it was all-in on the deal," said Scott. "There was no second-guessing with him. As I was going into my junior year, he decided to change things up to compete with the Florida States and Southern Cals of the world. He said, 'We've researched all of this, and we're going to go with it.' The result was no looking back. He was determined to prove to people that it would work."

Osborne was bold in his approach. He had a vision of how things would play out as those three national championships in his final four seasons reflect.

"Coach always had goals established for us so we could achieve them during the week of practice," Welniak said. "Then he had goals for the game as well. That way we all knew what was expected of us."

Welniak was from tiny Elyria, Nebraska, and went to high school in nearby Ord. He earned three letters at Nebraska, primarily for his special-teams play – though he also saw action at linebacker. His teammates thought enough of him that he was voted a co-captain as a senior in 1987, a unique honor for a special-teams player.

Osborne "was able to keep his composure in difficult times," said Welniak. "Tom was definitely a strategist and always thought ahead on the implications of his decisions. As a result, most of his decisions were the right ones."

He also "empowered his position coaches to make a lot of decisions on their own. He had a great staff and gave them the freedom to see what they could deliver," Welniak said.

As developed elsewhere in this book, Osborne believed in delegating responsibility.

"Coach was a visionary," said Mark Moravec, a senior in 1982, when the Huskers would have played for a national championship if not for a controversial finish at Penn State, which illustrated Osborne's composure and character. "He had the ability to look at a situation and pre-determine what the outcome would be. At halftime, he'd tell us something like, 'Don't retaliate; just keep hitting hard.' Things would work out exactly as he told us."

Moravec would seem to be a visionary in his description of Osborne's vision. Some 14 years later, with Nebraska trailing Miami 10-7 at halftime of the 1995 Orange Bowl game, Osborne told his players they were better conditioned and would wear down Miami. He also told them that if they could maintain their composure and not retaliate, the Hurricanes would draw a penalty that would significantly affect the game's outcome.

Miami had increased its lead to 17-7 early in the second half when a Hurricane pushed Nebraska defensive tackle Christian Peter after the whistle. Peter was among the Huskers least likely to walk away from such a challenge, but he dropped his arms, and the Miami player drew a 15-yard personal-foul penalty that moved the ball back to the Hurricanes' 4-yard line. On the next play, Nebraska outside linebacker Dwayne Harris sacked Miami quarterback Frank Costa in the end zone for a safety.

More important than the two points, perhaps, the play helped shift momentum in Nebraska's favor. Plus, it reinforced the Huskers' belief in their coach and what he told them.

Moravec, who walked on from Aquinas High School in David City, Nebraska, where he also was an all-state basketball player, earned three letters as a reserve fullback at Nebraska. He started one game his senior year. "Coach could read people very well," said Moravec. "He'd sit and visit with a player and could read between the lines and discover who you really were. Tom got his share of top-notch players, but never at the same level as other football powers. He was able to put together championship teams because he knew what made players tick and how to develop them to their full potential. He was a very effective communicator. We always had a clear understanding of what he wanted accomplished."

Walk-ons played an important role in Osborne's success, and again, they illustrated his leadership ability on several levels, including vision and boldness. Because of the limitations of population and geography, walk-ons helped to level the playing field in recruiting.

In 1974, as mentioned earlier, the NCAA reduced the number of scholarships allowed in a given year from 45 to 30. Two years later, Osborne began holding back a handful of the allotted 30 scholarships to award to walk-ons who had worked their way up the depth chart to the top units. And though, true walk-ons such as Krenk, those who just showed up looking for a chance, were still commonplace, Nebraska began evaluating walk-ons as it would scholarship recruits. "With the new screenings we have for walk-ons, we don't have any mediocre players," Husker freshman coach Frank Solich told the *Lincoln* (Nebraska) *Star* in 1979. "No matter who you put in there, they're pretty good athletes."

Isaiah Hipp had already established himself among the best running backs in Husker history at that point. He was among those walk-ons who weren't recruited. And his story was among the first to be recounted when the subject of walk-ons during the Osborne era was discussed.

Hipp, who was from Chapin, South Carolina, had received recruiting interest from top programs across the country before a collarbone injury sidelined him during his senior year in high school. If South Carolina had offered him a scholarship, he would have accepted. But it didn't, and neither did any of the other schools that had shown an interest in him before the injury.

So Hipp spent the price of a postage stamp (13 cents at the time) and recruited Nebraska, you might say, sending a form-letter questionnaire to the university and then following up by borrowing the price of a plane ticket from a friend in order to fly to Lincoln for the start of fall classes – he had never been on a plane. Borrowing the money for a ticket was a reflection of his belief in himself because he and a sister were raised by their great-grandmother; he certainly didn't have the money to walk on, especially so far from home. He planned to cover tuition costs with a Basic Economic Opportunity Grant (BEOG), a federal grant for which he qualified because Nebraska hadn't recruited him. In fact, like Krenk, Hipp had to ask Osborne if he could walk on. And as in Krenk's case, Osborne told Hipp if he was accepted for admission by the university, he could come out for the team.

Hipp picked Nebraska mostly because he had seen the Huskers on television, in a game against Oklahoma. Plus, by 1975, his freshman year, Nebraska was starting to build a reputation for being a haven for walk-ons. And his success enhanced that reputation. During his sophomore year, before he had earned a scholarship, he rushed for a school-record 254 yards in a 31-13 victory against Indiana, and Husker sports information director Don Bryant began referring to him as "collegiate football's most famous walk on." Bryant also used his initials I.M. (Isaiah Moses) to enhance the image.

But Hipp didn't really need the image enhancement. His numbers sufficed. In 12 games, counting the Liberty Bowl, he rushed for a school-record 1,353 yards and 10 touchdowns as a sophomore, adding another 1,000-yard season as a junior. Though hampered by injuries his senior year, he still finished as the leading rusher in Nebraska history and left as a fourth-round NFL draft pick.

Hipp credits Osborne with his success. "Coach carried himself with a sense of certainty but never cockiness," said Hipp. "He didn't want to be the center of attention. But attention always centered on him. He was a father figure to us. He had a way about him and a subtle sense of humor that drew people to him. I still chuckle about things Coach would say, and that was 30 years ago."

After a brief time in the NFL, Hipp returned to Nebraska with Osborne's encouragement, to finish a degree and do career counseling with athletes as well as at the Lincoln Regional Center.

"Coach always had a sense of the person he was dealing with," Hipp said. "He treated everyone with kindness, compassion and empathy." Such people skills are the focus of another chapter.

In 1981, nearly 90 players walked-on at Nebraska, with a dozen of them earning at least two letters during their careers, and in 1982, the freshman-junior varsity team included more than 70 walk-ons. Osborne called walk-ons the "salvation" of the program, explaining: "We have to work harder than anyone else on walk-on players because we're the only school consistently in the Top 10 with a sparsely populated area in a 200-mile radius."

Osborne didn't differentiate between walk-ons and scholarship players. "He was fair and treated us all the same," said Dr. Jeffrey Tomjack, a Husker safety in the mid-1980s. "A lot of walk-ons knew that they were every bit as much in the big picture as the highly recruited players."

Tomjack didn't walk on. He was a scholarship recruit. But he understood the walk-on mentality because he came from a small town in northeast Nebraska, Ewing, and had to delay his enrollment for a year because of reconstructive knee surgery.

"Coach taught us about persevering, keep getting up because tomorrow is another day. I remember looking at my first depth chart. I was down there at No. 12 on the list. But we had been taught to keep hanging around, put in the work, and you'll get your chance. Then when you do, make it happen," Tomjack said. He was, in effect, describing his own Husker career.

Though he was never a full-time starter, Tomjack earned three letters despite more knee problems and distinguished himself in the classroom as well as on the field. His junior season he was described in the Husker media guide as perhaps "the best alternate defensive back in the Big Eight." He started two games and was in the regular rotation.

"Osborne is such an unassuming man and a gentleman all the way," said Tomjack. "He is courteous to everyone because he thinks of himself as just a regular guy."

That helped explain his affinity for walk-ons, as did his brief NFL career, which "exposed me to a more sophisticated brand of football and taught me something about competition and perseverance and hanging in there," said Osborne, who was the 222nd player selected in the 12-team NFL draft following his career at Hastings College. "That's,

I think, one reason I could relate pretty well to walk-ons because a lot of our walk-ons were in about the same boat I was in.

"In pro football terminology, I guess, I was almost a walk-on. So I've appreciated the work ethic and willingness to sacrifice of the walk-on players."

Ryan Held walked on in 1993, following an all-state career as a wide receiver and defensive back at Blue Valley North High School in Overland Park, Kansas. Though he didn't play enough to earn a letter at Nebraska, he contributed to Osborne's three national championships, working as a scout-team quarterback, a back-up split end and special-teams player, and in 1997, an undergraduate assistant coach – Osborne gave him that opportunity after he suffered a career-ending injury two games into the 1996 season. Held is now the head football coach at Highland (Kansas) Community College.

"It could be the maintenance guy, a walk-on, or a fourth-stringer, Coach treated them all the same," Held said. "Every single person with the football program felt a part of it. They never felt isolated because Coach included everyone and got them on the same page.

"His communication skills were tremendous with all different types of athletes. It didn't matter whether it was an inner-city kid from Los Angeles or a farm boy from Geneva, Nebraska, Coach knew how to motivate and mold them so they'd be on the same page and do things the 'Nebraska way.' "

Held was a solid student, as was Darin Erstad, who returned to Nebraska and is now the Husker baseball coach. Erstad was recruited to play baseball, so he was technically a football walk-on. After his sophomore season, in which he earned first-team All-Big Eight honors, he tried out for the football team as a punter and place-kicker. He averaged 41.2 yards per punt to earn second-team all-conference recognition, as well as backing up as a place-kicker, making 10-of-10 extra-points and three field goals. He also was credited with four tackles on special teams. Then he returned to baseball. He was a first-team All-American and Big Eight Co-Player of the Year and the No. 1 overall pick in the 1995 Major League Baseball Draft.

Erstad played 14 years in the majors. He was a two-time All-Star, a three-time Gold Glove winner and Silver Slugger Award winner. He batted .352 during the World Series run of the Los Angeles Angels of Anaheim in 2002.

"When I think of Coach Osborne, I think of consistency. He knew the name of every player, from All-American to fifth-year walk-on," Erstad said, echoing Held. "He set the same high standard for everyone in the classroom and on the practice field. All of that was non-negotiable with Tom. I'm trying to apply those same principles today with my baseball players."

What Travis Turner has to say about Osborne would fit in just about any chapter in this book. Turner walked on from Scottsbluff, Nebraska, worked his way up the depth chart and started the last half of his junior season in 1984. He went into his senior season No. 1 on the depth chart but lost the starting job and played as a back-up, never complaining. His focus was always the team rather than himself. He's the executive director at Life Partners Christian Ministries in Scottsdale, Arizona, now.

"Coach always had a bigger picture in mind all the time," said Turner. "He was always concerned with building the program by working through the lives of others. Football was just a piece of the puzzle; it was really about life and life lessons. It was about the process and who you were becoming.

"Coach was a man of vision. He imparted that vision subtly and without pressure. I never saw him lose his temper or swear at a player. He was never demeaning, and he'd never embarrass a player or assistant coach. He honored the spirit of others. Many a time he put an arm around you and spoke to you quietly and respectfully."

Turner also spent one season as a graduate assistant under Osborne. "There was never any variance with what he said and what he lived," Turner said. "He always considered others above himself. It was never about elevating himself and always about elevating others. He was always a man of his word. Tom Osborne changed my life. I'm in full-time ministry and trying to give back what I've been given."

Vision, people skills, communication, serving heart, competence, consistency; Turner can testify to all those elements of leadership, in addition to the boldness of the walk-on program.

Consistency? "As a leader, Coach was always steady and consistent with his demeanor. He understood that football is an emotional game and that there are many highs and lows," Andy Means said. "He wanted us to be on an even keel, just as he was."

Means, a second-generation Husker (his dad, Arden Means, was a letterman in the late 1940s), walked on from Holdrege, Nebraska, and started for three seasons at cornerback. He was a first-team Academic All-Big Eight honoree as a senior in 1980.

"Coach never swore," said Means, the head coach at Omaha's Millard South High School. "He'd get angry at times, but it was always specific anger. He was not a coach who ranted and railed at his players. He wanted to win championships, but to do that, his teams had to play with consistency every Saturday. Our ups and downs had to be kept to a minimum.

"To me, Tom Osborne is a great man and a great and honest leader."

Bruce Dunning not only walked on, he also was from out-of-state, Arvada, Colorado, which meant he could have gotten discouraged before getting on the field at linebacker as a junior. He was Means' teammate as a senior in 1978, a starter who finished second on the team in tackles.

"Coach Osborne was a leader who stood by the courage of his convictions and did not waver," said Dunning, who played an important role in Nebraska's 17-14 upset of No. 1-ranked Oklahoma in 1978, recounted elsewhere in this book. "He never made a big deal about his religious faith, but all of us knew exactly where he stood. His message was very clear, so you knew what he expected from you. As a walk-on, I had to prove myself initially, but after that Coach treated me like any other player."

Matt Turman, a walk-on from Wahoo, Nebraska, became a fan favorite, earning the nickname "Turmanator" after stepping in to start at quarterback at Kansas State his sophomore year in 1994, when Tommie Frazier was sidelined by blood clots and Brook Berringer was suffering from a collapsed lung. Turman was coached by his dad, Tim Turman, in high school. He wasn't a big guy, listed at 5-foot-11 and 165 pounds, but he was determined. "We knew that Coach Osborne worked extremely hard to do his best for us. We responded with the same type of attitude and approach," Turman said.

"I'd sit in meetings and film sessions with him and hear him predict things that would happen in games, and it always seemed to happen that way. Coach worked so hard, studied film endlessly, and the game inside and out. It was very easy to buy into his game plan."

Turman draws up his own game plans now as head coach at Omaha's Skutt High School, where he also teaches history. "Coach cared more about his players than he did about himself," said Turman. "I try to do that with my players. He never asked anything of us that he wasn't willing to do himself. A perfect example would be his policy of no cussing, gambling or drinking. We knew he wouldn't do those things, so that made him a great leader by example. We could see that he practiced what he preached, every day."

That Osborne practiced what he preached was apparent in many ways.

"What I remember about Coach Osborne the most is what I think made him a great leader. He always had a sense of calm about him no matter what the situation was," said Keven Lightner, the offensive line coach for Frank Solich at Ohio. "Good or bad, he remained calm and confident. He made me feel if we just hung in there that everything would turn out in our favor. It usually did."

Lightner, an offensive tackle, weighed 230 pounds when he walked on out of high school in Hastings, Nebraska. He ran the 40-yard dash in 5.37 seconds and his vertical jump was 31½ inches. He weighed 285 pounds as a senior. His 40-yard dash time had dropped to :04.98 and his vertical jump had increased to 39½ inches. He also scored the highest of any Husker at the time on Epley's strength index. Those increases were reflected on the field. Lightner earned first-team All-Big Eight honors in 1987.

Cartier Walker was a junior in 1987, a walk-on defensive back all the way from Atlantic City, New Jersey. Walker earned two letters, playing almost exclusively on special teams.

Osborne "is still having an impact on me after all these years. When we played for him, he led by example. Everything he asked us to do he'd do himself," Walker said, repeating what Turman said. "Coach stressed to us that we were a reflection of the university for the rest of our lives. He was concerned about our futures and always asked us, 'Where do you see yourself three years from now?'"

You'll read more of this in the chapter that recounts the TeamMates program established by Osborne and his wife Nancy as well as the chapter focusing on his people skills.

"Coach and his staff were always prepared, which helped us be prepared for life," said Walker. "He was a father-figure to many of us who grew up without fathers. He shaped us up to be quality young men, who could be successful long after our football days.

"Coach knew everyone's name and still does, which is amazing when you consider the thousands of players he coached over 25 years. That showed how much he cared for us. It means a lot to go back to the university and have our old coach speak to all of us by name."

As Malcolm Moran wrote in *The New York Times* at the start of Walker's senior season, when the Huskers were preparing to open against Texas A&M in the Kickoff Classic at Giants Stadium in East Rutherford, New Jersey – Walker was going home – the effort of walk-ons provided the "physical and emotional backbone" of Nebraska's program under Osborne.

The 2009 documentary *Walk-Ons: Huskers' Edge* capsulizes the program and an aspect of Osborne's leadership that could be described by any of the seven principles that are the basis for this book.

Wisconsin Athletic Director, and former Badger coach, Barry Alvarez played linebacker for Nebraska (1965-67) under Bob Devaney, when Osborne was an assistant coach.

"Almost everything we did at Wisconsin, we stole from Nebraska, including the fabled walk-on program," Alvarez said. "I used the Nebraska blueprint. We analyzed what we could do and what we could consistently have and then we implemented our (recruiting) strategy.

"First, we kept the best in-state kids at home. Then we recruited the best players we could recruit to be a very physical, run-oriented team. And, finally, when we realized no one in the Big Ten was doing what Nebraska was doing with walk-ons, we went after it. Walk-ons were a big key to my success and still are to our program. For all the mistakes we make in recruiting, walk-ons are our erasers."

Chapter Four:

VISION: SEEING WAYS TO WIN

"When you watched him on the sideline, if you weren't playing, you could see that he was always a play ahead."

—**DAVE RIMINGTON** (1979-82) on Tom Osborne

A couple of weeks before the Oklahoma game in 1982, the Huskers began practicing the play. It involved quarterback Turner Gill throwing a pass, laterally, to wingback Irving Fryar, who was split wide to Gill's left. Gill was to bounce the ball, skip it if he could. Fryar would scoop up the ball and hesitate, then turn and toss the ball down the field to a receiver. If the play worked as designed, the receiver would be wide-open because the defense would relax, if only for an instant, thinking the ball was dead. As a lateral, however, the ball would be live, a fumble not an incomplete pass.

Dave Rimington, Nebraska's All-America center and senior co-captain, once recalled telling coach Tom Osborne at the time he hoped if the Huskers ever ran the play in a game they were either ahead by 100 points or behind by 100 points. Rimington was not a fan of the play.

As with most offensive linemen, Rimington preferred running plays. He wanted to come off the ball aggressively and attack the defense, no holding back in pass protection, an approach that earned him the Outland Trophy as well as recognition as Big Eight Offensive Player of the Year the previous season. That's right, no need to rub your eyes and look again. The center from Omaha was the conference offensive player of the year in 1981, according to both major wire services.

That he didn't repeat in 1982 wasn't surprising, either. Teammate Mike Rozier, a junior I-back, earned that honor, as well as consensus All-America recognition, after rushing for nearly 1,700 yards and 15 touchdowns. A center couldn't compete with that. Even so, Rimington did all right in the recognition department, earning the Lombardi Award as well as an unprecedented second Outland Trophy. He also earned unanimous All-America honors for a second time, and he was a first-team Academic All-American for a second consecutive year, the definitive student-athlete.

There's more about Osborne's emphasis on academics, an important aspect of his ability as a leader throughout this book. So back to the trick play for which Rimington had no use.

Oklahoma came to Memorial Stadium with a No. 11 ranking in the Associated Press poll on the Friday after Thanksgiving in 1982. The Huskers were No. 3, the only blemish on their record a controversial 27-24 loss at Penn State in the third game of the season. Osborne called the trick play early in the second quarter, on the series following a field goal that had given the Sooners a 10-7 lead.

Nebraska lined up at its own 49-yard line, first-and-10. Tight end Mitch Krenk brought in the play from the sideline. Rimington was unhappy. He looked Krenk's way and said something best described as a disbelieving question: "We're not running that blankety-blank play?"

Only he didn't say "blankety-blank." Krenk responded that he was just the messenger. He also would be the receiver on the play.

Gill bounced the ball to Fryar, who scooped it up. He didn't have time to sell the fake, under pressure from two Oklahoma defenders, including strong safety Greg Lowell, who was closing quickly. Fryar said afterward he couldn't see Krenk crossing over the middle. He just got rid of the ball quickly, grasping it near one end rather than near the middle, on the laces, because his hands weren't big enough to do so. That was the only way the ball would spiral instead of flutter.

The Sooner defensive backs weren't fooled either. Cornerback Scott Case was running with Krenk, who made a juggling, one-handed catch. "Luckily I made the catch of my life," Krenk would recall years later, adding with a laugh that Fryar's pass was well-thrown and the catch wouldn't have seemed so dramatic had he, Krenk, been able to run faster.

By the time Krenk was tackled, he was at the Oklahoma 14-yard line. Three plays later, fullback Doug Wilkening charged into the end zone and the Huskers had regained the lead, on the way to a dramatic 28-24 victory that gave Nebraska an outright Big Eight championship and Orange Bowl bid.

Even though, years later, Rimington still maintained the play had rarely worked during practice leading up to the Oklahoma game, it confirmed what he believed about Osborne. "From that point on, I just said: 'That's why he's a coach and I'm a player,'" Rimington said.

On the surface, Osborne might have seemed conservative in his offensive approach. His early teams were balanced between pass and run, with quarterbacks who weren't inclined to tuck the ball and run, as is recounted elsewhere in this book. For his final 20 seasons, however, the Husker offense was run-oriented. Nebraska led the nation in rushing 11 times in those 20 seasons and ranked lower than third only once – when it was fourth. The Huskers also ranked first or second in scoring eight times in those seasons and were in the top 10 all but twice during his entire head-coaching career.

Such numbers quantify his vision, his offensive imagination, and reflect the reason his players had confidence in what he told them, as Rimington's comment about the bounced lateral illustrates. Osborne was his own offensive coordinator for 25 seasons. He understood the X's and O's of football, and he was able to communicate them to his players. "I think he was more creative than most people give him credit for," Rimington said. "When the opportunity presented itself, he ran some interesting and creative plays, such as the 'Bummerooski,' 'fumblerooski' and 'bouncerooski.' "

A radio announcer described the bounced-lateral play as the "bouncerooski." And the play was preserved on a glass mug marketed by the *Lincoln* (Nebraska) *Star* afterward. The mug included an etching of the first couple of paragraphs from a newspaper story the next day. Krenk has one of the mugs, purchased by his grandmother.

The spelling of the play varies: "bouncerooski," "bouncerooosky" and "bouncerooskie." It was preceded by the "Bummerooski" and "fumblerooski," also trick plays, with the same variant endings, borrowed from other coaches and used by Osborne. Colorado had used the "bouncerooski" several years earlier, Osborne said following the Oklahoma game in 1982. He was constantly studying film, breaking it down, and not just from college games. He would get ideas from high school films as well, when he was evaluating recruits. Osborne's approach was as blue-collar as his Nebraska roots. He would not be out-worked and neither would his teams.

Much of Osborne's coaching vision wasn't apparent from the stands, but it created headaches for defensive coordinators. The Huskers ran plays from a variety of formations, with often-subtle adjustments.

When he pulled out a trick play, such as the "bouncerooski," that was cause for comment.

He called for the "Bummerooski" in the 1975 Missouri game at Columbia, Missouri, where his first loss as a head coach had come two years before. The Tigers came to Lincoln the next year and won again. Detractors of the young coach pointed to those losses and back-to-back losses to Oklahoma as evidence Athletic Director Bob Devaney had picked the wrong assistant to succeed him.

The "Bummerooski" was named for coach Bum Phillips, who was credited with devising the play when he was an assistant to Bear Bryant at Texas A&M. Jerry Moore, the first assistant not on staff that Osborne hired after being named head coach, had brought the play with him from Southern Methodist, where he had been an assistant to Hayden Fry.

Nebraska led Missouri 10-0 with 1:46 remaining before halftime, facing fourth down at the Tigers' 40-yard line. Randy Lessman was the punter, with three running backs in front of him, near the line of scrimmage, aligned in a triangle. Tony Davis was directly behind the center, with Monte Anthony and John O'Leary a step ahead of him, Anthony to his left, O'Leary to his right.

Davis took the snap, pushed the ball from behind, through O'Leary's legs, then turned as if to hand it to Anthony, who was running to his right. The play appeared to be a reverse, with all of the Huskers, including Lessman, also running to the right. O'Leary cradled the ball and delayed, then ran to the left, 40 yards untouched to the end zone. The game was televised nationally by ABC, and the television cameras, like the Missouri defenders and the fans at Faurot Field, didn't focus on O'Leary until he was well on his way. Nebraska won the game 30-7.

Four seasons later, the Huskers would run the "fumblerooski" for the first time. More than the others, that play, a guard-around, came to represent Osborne's offensive imagination.

Osborne called it twice during the 1979 Oklahoma game at Norman, Oklahoma. Senior John Havekost, the left guard, ran it first, gaining 11 yards. But junior Randy Schleusener, the right guard, drew most of the attention afterward because he ran 15 yards for a touchdown with 4:43 remaining in the 17-14 Husker loss. Nebraska's football media guide the next year referred to Schleusener as "probably the most famous guard in college football for the 1980 season." The play had made Schleusener's name "a household word among college football fans," the entry in the guide said.

Havekost, first-team All-Big Eight in 1979, was listed at 6-foot-4 and 230 pounds, Schleusener at 6-foot-7, 242 pounds. Both were lanky. Both had good hands. And both could run.

According to Rimington, a redshirted freshman back-up in 1979, the "fumblerooski" never worked consistently in practice either. He became the starter the next year, and whenever he'd practice the play, he said, he'd end up kicking the ball away as he moved to block a defender.

Osborne never called the play with Rimington at center. But he pulled it out in the 1984 Orange Bowl game against Miami, described earlier in the chapter about Osborne's career.

The Huskers had fallen behind 17-0 in the first quarter, in marked contrast to the regular season, when they had outscored opponents by a combined 139-19 in the first quarters of 12 games, and they needed an offensive spark. Senior Dean Steinkuhler provided it.

Steinkuhler, the Outland Trophy and Lombardi Award winner in 1983, was the right guard. He was 6-foot-3 and 270 pounds, but he could run 40 yards in under 5 seconds. Specifically, he had run that distance in team testing in 4.87 seconds, timed electronically. Mark Traynowicz, Rimington's successor at center, snapped the ball to Gill, the quarterback, who set the ball on the ground. Steinkuhler picked it up, running to the left, and when he built up a head of steam, there was no stopping him, even though two Miami defenders were in position to try. The touchdown run covered 19 yards.

Osborne wouldn't call the "fumblerooski" again until, appropriately perhaps, Halloween in 1992, against Colorado at Memorial Stadium. The Buffaloes came to Lincoln tied with Nebraska at No. 8 in the Associated Press rankings. The Huskers lined up third-and-4 at the Colorado 21-yard line, leading 17-7, with time running out in the first half. Right guard Will Shields, who would win the Outland Trophy that season, picked up the intentional fumble by quarterback Tommie Frazier, after taking the snap from Jim Scott, and carried the ball 16 yards to the 5-yard line. Three plays later, I-back Calvin Jones scored.

Following the 1992 season, the NCAA would change the rules, and the guard-around as Nebraska ran it, the "fumblerooski," was made illegal. The reason? It was too difficult to officiate. Years later, in discussing Osborne's imagination, Krenk would say: "They always say one of the attributes of a great coach is when they cause rules changes." He was referring specifically to the "fumblerooski," a memorable example of Osborne's unique vision.

Chuck Pool's name is linked to the "fumblerooski" in a unique way.

Rewind to the 1984 Orange Bowl game, described at length in the chapter that introduces Osborne, and specifically Dean Steinkuhler's touchdown run. Pool was an assistant in the Nebraska sports information office and NBC television, "after originally saying they had the spotters they needed, came rushing in full panic into the pressbox to ask me to come to the broadcast booth because the person they had lined up had no clue about us (the Huskers)," said Pool.

"Apparently, Don Criqui and John Brodie were about to kill the guy for screwing up. I had been in the advance meetings with them, so they knew who I was when I climbed in, which is how you had to get into the TV booth at the old Orange Bowl stadium."

Pool continued: "As it happened, I walked in just as we ran the fumblerooski play with Dean Steinkuhler, and I quickly scribbled down some info on the play for them. I was immortalized on the broadcast because Don said, 'Our man from Nebraska, Chuck Pool, tells us we have just seen the fumblerooski.' So the rest of the game, they were looking to me as a credible source."

More about that and how the game defined Osborne's leadership in a special way, but first, something about Pool, now the Assistant Athletics Director/Sports Information at Rice University.

He was a member of the Husker freshman football team in 1977. Guy Ingles, a former Husker, was Osborne's head freshman coach at the time. Pool has said he played enough to know that he had "reached the ceiling" of his athletic abilities.

"Four years later, while standing on the sideline at a Christmas Day practice as the Huskers prepared for Clemson on a sweltering Miami day, one of my former teammates saw me standing there in my coaching shorts and polo and said, 'You figured this thing out, didn't you? You're here with the rest of us, except you don't have to practice,'" Pool said.

"I only wish it was the result of some great vision."

Pool was a full-time assistant in the Nebraska sports information office by then. He began as a student assistant in the fall of 1979, Osborne's seventh season as head coach.

He left Nebraska in 1985 to work for the Houston Astros as an assistant director of public relations. He also was the first public relations director for the Miami Marlins before running his own sports-related public relations firm, promoting among other things, the Rotary Lombardi Award.

Pool's resume is significant here because not only has he been exposed to leadership in athletics but what he has done, and does, allows him to express what he has seen. So let's return to the 1984 Orange Bowl game against Miami and see how, through his eyes, it reflects Osborne the leader.

"I guess it comes down to his unflinching acceptance of the responsibility of making the tough decision," said Pool. "That breeds trust and confidence in those under his leadership."

Remember, Nebraska battled back and scored a touchdown with 48 seconds remaining to cut the score to 31-30. "When we scored the touchdown at the end, in the midst of all the drama and emotion, the one thing that people forget is that there was no lag in time between the TD and the decision to go for two," Pool said. "The way you see it in the various features that have been done, you miss the fact that it was total elation and then crushing dejection in less than 30 seconds. No timeouts, nothing. I was hanging on by a thread emotionally to not jump out of the (NBC) booth with joy when we scored.

"It had been a very long year for a young pup assistant SID who had to shepherd Mike Rozier through the weekly crush of Heisman demands, so winning this game was the only possible reward. But as Jeff Smith crossed the goal line, Don (Criqui) and John (Brodie) spun around and looked at me to see what I thought we would do. In the middle of all that commotion, all the surges of emotion, one thing was beyond question. And that was that Coach would go for two.

"I immediately held up two fingers, indicating we'd go for two, and both broadcasters dismissed me with the wave of their hand. But I pointed to the end zone, where we were already lining up to go for it. I knew because he (Osborne) did not operate in a world that thought in terms of tossing it to voters by kicking the point and tying. It was a massively complex and wide-ranging issue reduced to a very simple formula: We came to win. The rest of that play and the end of the game are a blur, to this day. I can tell you that even now, I can't watch the two-point conversion. Hurts too much."

That was Osborne's "unflinching acceptance of the responsibility of making the tough decision."

Eleven years later, Pool was in the stands at the Orange Bowl stadium – he worked for the Marlins then – when the Huskers defeated Miami to give Osborne his first national championship. His "greatest memory" of that night "was to see Turner Gill celebrating as he ran off the field," said Pool.

Gill was the quarterback who threw the two-point conversion pass that was deflected incomplete in the 1984 Orange Bowl game and he was Osborne's quarterbacks coach for all three of Osborne's national championships. "Turner and I became pretty good friends, and I knew at that moment, the stigma of that failed attempt had been muted, if not totally eliminated," Pool said.

"As a side note, one other thing lost in the recapturing of that epic ending is the near arrogance of running essentially a basic option play with your second-team back (Smith) on a fourth-and-long with the game, the national title and the legacy of being one of the greatest teams in history hanging in the balance," said Pool. "That reality struck me years later when I was watching the tape of the game – and shut it off after this play. It was telling that a man who was well-known for gimmick plays had, in this moment, chosen to go with what had gotten them there."

Such was Osborne's vision.

Pool didn't watch Osborne's handling of Lawrence Phillips, described elsewhere in this book, but that handling was in line with what Pool had seen 10 years before, when he was a sports information assistant. Osborne remained consistent. "He believed that he had one possible way to reach Lawrence, which was the goal to get on the field again," Pool said. "I will always believe that was his guiding belief in taking the stance he did, despite the firestorm that still lingers and will always be a footnote to his legacy. He made the decision he felt was right, and that decision was never made with an idea of how it would play in the court of public opinion.

"I always wondered how that trait would translate into politics when I first heard he was running. That is a field that is, in the end, the exact opposite of this very simple but very powerful characteristic of Coach. He is the antithesis of a politician."

Osborne was part of the Nebraska delegation in the press box at Rosenblatt Stadium (now gone) in Omaha for the NCAA College World Series when President George W. Bush was there to throw out the first pitch. "I asked him (Osborne) whom he preferred: Sports writers or political writers. And he gave a little smile and asked: 'Now why would you ask that?' Funny thing was when President Bush walked into the press box, he (Bush) looked around and asked: 'Baseball writers?' To which everyone acknowledged, and he (Bush) said, 'The best kind.' One was still a coach at heart, the other was a politician."

J. Dennis Hastert can speak to Osborne the politician. Hastert was the Republican Speaker of the House of Representatives (1999-2007) when Osborne served in Congress. "Tom didn't push himself on people, but he had a strong sense of confidence about him," said Hastert.

"He knew what he was doing because he was very studious and always did his homework on issues. On his various projects, Tom kept at it until he got things done. He could convince people with common sense, and people loved him for that. He's just a plain, low-key, Midwestern good guy."

University of Nebraska-Lincoln Chancellor Harvey Perlman says much the same thing, though in a different way. "First, a disclaimer; I am not a student of what makes a good leader," Perlman said. "I recognize it when I see it, but I am skeptical of much of the literature in the field. The only description of leadership I've read that makes some sense is Jim Collins' description of a Level 5 leader in *Good to Great*. Tom certainly displays many of the characteristics identified by Collins. As Collins observes: 'Level 5 leaders embody a paradoxical mix of personal humility and professional will. They are ambitious, to be sure, but ambitious first and foremost for the company not themselves.'

"He also mentions 'compelling modesty, self-effacing, and understated' as attributes of a Level 5 leader. And such a leader is 'fanatically driven, infected with an incurable need to produce sustained results.' Also, 'workmanlike diligence – more plow horse than show horse.' Seems to me, these accurately describe Tom."

Osborne's sustained results in athletics are reflected not only in his Hall of Fame coaching record but also in what he accomplished as athletic director. In addition to the expansion of Memorial Stadium to a capacity of more than 90,000 and the building, in partnership with the City of Lincoln, of a new arena for basketball as well as basketball practice facilities, an $8.7 million Student Life Complex was dedicated on Sept. 11, 2010. The 50,000 square-foot complex will support 600 Husker student-athletes.

Perlman hired Osborne as interim athletic director on Oct. 16, 2007, replacing Steve Pederson. Osborne said at the news conference to announce his return, he had accepted the job because Perlman had asked. At a Sept. 26, 2102 news conference to announce he would be retiring effective Jan. 1, 2013, Osborne said: "I'm honored that he (Perlman) would've asked me to do this job five years ago. At the time that he asked me, I wasn't sure whether it was a good idea or not. Hopefully, it's worked out well."

No one could dispute that it had worked out well.

"He certainly stabilized the department," Perlman said, also at the news conference. "He's hired some very promising coaches. He's brought our facilities to a new level. I think it's important that the first facility he moved on with was Life Skills and academics. I think that tells us a little about his views and the culture of our athletic department. It was obviously fun to work with him in moving Nebraska to the Big Ten. It wouldn't have happened without his support, and that was a good time for both of us."

As Perlman quoted Collins in *Good to Great*, Osborne's personal humility was in marked contrast to his professional will. "I've had the opportunity to travel with him and work with him, and there are people who you can admire from a distance, and then you get up close and see all the warts and everything else. That's not true with my experience with Tom," said Perlman.

"It's been really fun to interview head coaches with him and to see the kind of national respect and awe they have with his reputation and position in the coaching community. It's been great to see him, and in some ways sympathetic to him, to have to walk from one place in a foreign stadium to another. A walk that would usually take 5 minutes takes 20 because people want to stop for an autograph or to say hello. I think we probably don't recognize in Nebraska the tremendous amount of respect (for Osborne) nationally, not just in intercollegiate athletics but in other venues as well."

Jim McClurg recognizes it. "Tom Osborne is a Nebraska and USA treasure," said McClurg, the Chairman of the University of Nebraska Board of Regents.

"He leads by example and by teaching. Fortunately he has been in a position to exemplify and teach leadership to thousands through his coaching and leadership of UNL athletics and his lifetime willingness to be available and accessible to the public. Among the many great victories and recognition have been thousands of small, uncelebrated acts that total to a career of leading and creating a culture of leadership. I believe Tom's leadership is based on some core values that guide much of what he believes and does – they include his faith, his belief in the potential of young people, the value and reward of focused effort and work, and a forgiving nature."

McClurg continued: "Tom has lived and coached with clearly articulated goals, with accountability and discipline. For example, having a season team goal to be the best conditioned and prepared to play to the team's goal versus a goal of just 'to win.' His career has exemplified what Bobby Knight meant when he said 'the will to win is important, but more important is the will to prepare to win.'"

Anyone who played for Osborne would attest to that. He emphasized preparation and accepted the results. If his team prepared properly and played to the best of its ability, winning would follow.

Osborne personally handled the preparation of his quarterbacks. He began meeting with the quarterbacks in the late 1960s, in fact, while he was the receivers coach. He had a special connection with them, none more so than Gill, for whom he was a groomsman at Gill's wedding.

"If he wasn't the coach, I probably wouldn't have been at Nebraska; I'm almost certain of that," Gill said during an interview years later, when he returned to coach Osborne's quarterbacks.

"I could trust him," said Gill. "I guess that was a key thing in my mind when I was being recruited and even when I was coming back as a coach. 'I could trust this man.'"

Gill's recruitment out of high school in Fort Worth, Texas, illustrated the point. Gill grew up following Oklahoma and figured if the Sooners offered him a scholarship, he would accept. But the Sooners did offer a scholarship, and he didn't accept. Rather he became a Husker and helped to change the way Osborne's quarterbacks played the game.

"Tom Osborne is a great leader for many reasons," said Gill, now the head football coach at Liberty University in Lynchburg, Virginia. "When I think of a leader, I always think of what it is that makes people want to follow that person. It is easy to follow Tom because he is genuine and he has a tremendous amount of integrity. There are a couple of examples that stand out in my mind of Tom's integrity during my time as a player and a coach."

To understand the first of those examples requires some background.

Gill played with Nebraska's freshman team, as most newcomers did. Not many freshmen played with the varsity during Osborne's 25 seasons. So Gill wasn't unique. He led the freshman team to a 5-0 record and set school freshman records for total offense and pass-completion percentage. His skills were such, however, that Osborne talked with him about moving up to the varsity. Gill told Osborne he didn't think he was ready for varsity competition, a reflection of his maturity.

Now about that first example to which Gill referred. "When I was a sophomore, I kept telling Tom that I thought I should be the starting quarterback," Gill said. "He would always tell me that I would get my chance after the other, more experienced, players got their chance. Even though it wasn't what I wanted to hear, I respected him for telling me the truth.

"He was true to what he said. I got my chance after they had theirs."

Gill, who began his sophomore season (in 1981) third on the depth chart behind a senior and another sophomore who had red-shirted, made the most of his opportunity. In his first start, in the fifth game against Colorado, he tied a school record by throwing four touchdown passes.

He never relinquished the starting job, though a foot injury late in the season forced him to the sideline and he missed two games, including an Orange Bowl loss to Clemson. Gill's record as the Huskers' starter was 28-2, including 20-0 in the Big Eight. He was a first-team all-conference selection three times and finished fourth in voting for the Heisman Trophy in 1983.

The Heisman winner was teammate Mike Rozier.

Gill also played one season of baseball at Nebraska – he was a second-round draft pick of the Chicago White Sox out of high school as a shortstop and was drafted again by the New York Yankees while at Nebraska. He played professionally in the Cleveland Indians' farm system, three seasons, following two seasons with the Montreal Concordes in the Canadian Football League.

Gill began a coaching career at North Texas as a volunteer assistant. He was a grad assistant at Nebraska and then SMU before Osborne hired him as quarterbacks coach in 1992.

"When I coached under Tom, he made sure that we knew as a coaching staff that we stood by our word," Gill said. "On occasion, someone would regret offering a scholarship to a student-athlete, but Tom said that we would not take away a scholarship offer in order to gain an advantage. He taught us as coaches that singularly, or as a collective group, we were only as good as our word."

Gill coached the Husker quarterbacks for 12 years, including Osborne's three national championship seasons, and six years under Osborne's successor, Frank Solich. Bill Callahan, Solich's successor, retained Gill as receivers coach, but after one season, Gill resigned with an eye on being a head coach. Before going to Liberty University, he was the head coach at Buffalo and Kansas.

His announcement at a news conference in early December of 2004 that he was leaving Nebraska was emotional. "Twenty-four years ago I came to play football at the University of Nebraska because of a vision of an outstanding leader, coach and Christian man named Tom Osborne," he said. "I came back to coach under him because of the same vision."

Vision; Dave Humm used that same word. "Tom was the kind of leader you want to latch onto and follow," he said. "When things are falling apart, he's not going to be thrown off-track. His vision was so clear and his sense of direction was impeccable. Tom handled his success with such class and humility. He shuns any credit and always says, 'It's about the team we have.'

"And here he is at 75 still giving back and contributing to his beloved Cornhuskers."

Humm knows about class and humility, qualities that characterize his life after football. He has dealt with the ravages of multiple sclerosis since 1988, 15 years after finishing a record-setting career at Nebraska. He finished as the No. 1 passer in school history, throwing for 5,236 yards and 42 touchdowns and earning All-America honors as a senior in 1974. In all, he held a dozen Nebraska records and four Big Eight Conference records, as well as the NCAA record for consecutive pass completions in a game.

Humm was a 5-star recruit before the Internet, coming out of high school in Las Vegas, Nevada. He was a three-year starter at Nebraska, his first season Devaney's last as coach. He also spent 10 seasons in the NFL, most of them as a back-up for the Oakland and Los Angeles Raiders.

Osborne "had the ability to rise above the masses," Humm said. "He was never worried about others' opinions or what was written about him. Tom was completely focused on his teams and his players. He could rise above the outside chatter and that included people questioning what he was doing.

"His focus was that great. Tom was mentally tough. All the outside distractions just rolled off his shoulders. He knew what was important and didn't let outside things distract him."

Vince Ferragamo stepped into the quarterback mix at Nebraska the season after Humm left for the NFL as a fifth-round pick of the Raiders. The Huskers had recruited Ferragamo in high school in Los Angeles; he even signed a Big Eight letter-of-intent with Nebraska. But he opted to go to California (over Stanford) and played two seasons with the Bears, competing for time with Steve Bartkowski. Ferragamo started much of his sophomore year, ahead of Bartkowski, but when coach Mike White decided to alternate the two, Ferragamo decided to transfer to Nebraska.

Ferragamo, who sat out Humm's senior season under NCAA transfer rules, began the 1975 season as a back-up to Terry Luck but became the starter in conference play. As a senior, he earned All-America honors from the *Football News,* passing for 2,254 yards and a school-record of 22 touchdowns. He also was a first-team Academic All-American.

"First of all, I think the world of Tom Osborne," said Ferragamo. "His biggest asset was his poised demeanor. He was always in control, self-confident and knowledgeable. He has a huge appetite for new, innovative ideas, both for offense and defense. Preparation was key for Tom. No one out-worked us or out-coached us. We were always ahead of the game. He was always a step ahead of the competition."

Again, an aspect of Osborne's vision.

"As solid and fundamental as we were, we always had a flair for the unexpected. We had a new wrinkle each week," Ferragamo said. "We would beat teams with our power offense, and then when things got close, we would surprise them with the unexpected."

Ferragamo was the quarterback in the 1975 Missouri game, in which the Huskers ran the "Bummerooski," as described at the beginning of this chapter.

Osborne "always had trust in his coaches and players. In return, he got the most out of everyone," said Ferragamo. "Above all else, he treated each and every one fairly and with respect. He believed that the total team was equal to the sum of its parts, that everyone contributed, big or small, and every phase was important to winning. He was committed to winning and so were his coaches. Tom learned from Bob Devaney and carried the torch. Bob had faith and trust in Tom and so did we."

Ferragamo played 10 seasons in the NFL, with the Rams, Bills and Packers, as well as one season in the Canadian Football League with the Montreal Alouettes. He led the Rams to Super Bowl XIV. He's a successful businessman in southern California, owning Touchdown Real Estate and EndZone Mortgage.

"We are all grateful for Tom and his wife Nancy, for their years of service to Nebraska," Ferragamo said. "Having Tom Osborne as my coach left a positive impression on me that I will carry the rest of my life. God bless you, Tom."

What better endorsement of a leader?

Malcolm Moran, the first Knight Chair in Sports Journalism and Society in the College of Communications at Penn State, dealt with Osborne during a distinguished sports writing career that began at *Newsday* and included 20 years at *The New York Times*, as well as time at the *Chicago Tribune* and *USA Today*. He is a member of the Football Writers Association of America Board of Directors.

"As a leader, Tom was so understated compared to so many of his peers," said Moran. "Normally with head coaches you think of fire and brimstone, but Tom was just the opposite. He was so cerebral and his teams played that way – always under control and poised. That came from Tom's approach. The emotion came from his senior leadership in the locker room. Tom was in charge of the X's and O's. It was fun to watch him calling plays and luring the other team into a trap.

"Tom might attack with an X and then spring Y on them."

Moran will testify to Osborne's humility. "Tom didn't call attention to himself and never sought credit for himself. He was about the strategic element and put his players in position to succeed.

"Tom and Dean Smith shared many of the same qualities – their cerebral approach, attention to detail and an understated approach to leadership. Both had tough acts to follow. Bob Devaney at Nebraska and Frank McGuire at North Carolina were both dynamic and colorful leaders, so Tom and Dean were both placed in intense, glaring spotlights."

"Whoa, Nellie!" Every college football fan of a certain age grew up with Keith Jackson, the voice of college football on ABC television for 40 seasons. Jackson has a special connection to Nebraska, due to his friendship with the Huskers' equally legendary sports information director, Don Bryant.

Bryant was Nebraska's sports information director, under different titles – the last of which was Associate Athletic Director for Communications – for all but Osborne's final season as coach, when he had the title Sports Information Director Emeritus. Bryant joined the staff in 1963, Devaney's second season, after covering the Huskers as sports editor of the *Lincoln* (Nebraska) *Star*.

Bryant was presented the Football Writers Association of America Bert McGrane Award in 1998 at the College Football Hall of Fame in South Bend, Indiana. He is a past president of the College Sports Information Directors of America and received the Arch Ward Memorial Award for outstanding service to the profession. And those are only a small number of his accomplishments.

The pressbox at Memorial Stadium bears his name and includes his signature red-plaid sport coat, framed, in the lounge area. Osborne "delegated the SID department to me and let me do my job," said Bryant, who is known by "Fox," his nickname from high school in Lincoln.

"He never climbed on my back."

Jackson was consulted when Nebraska up-graded its pressbox facilities and among his suggestions was including a restroom in the television broadcast booth. That suggestion led to "The Keith Jackson Toilet Facility," dedicated on Sept. 11, 1999, when Nebraska defeated California 45-0.

Jackson has done the introduction to the Huskers' pre-game "Tunnel Walk," shown on Memorial Stadium's massive HuskerVision screens, as well as a recorded segment for the video shown prior to the stadium's NCAA-record 300th consecutive sellout on Sept. 27, 2009.

"Tom was tall, so you always knew when he walked into the room," Jackson said of Osborne. "He'd walk in and speak quietly as he made his way around the room. Not a lot of talking and no slapping of palms. Tom would get his politicking done with the least amount of noise of any coach I ever met. When I got to Lincoln to set up,

Tom would see me in the morning, and in 15 minutes, we'd cover everything. I had it in my pocket and that was it. The man was quiet and efficient."

He also was imaginative in his approach to the game. "Tom was a riverboat gambler. He was not afraid to throw a bomb when it was least expected or run a reverse or double-reverse when the opponent had no idea Tom would run that play," said Jackson. "Tom lives an impeccable life because he believes in all the right values. I've never heard anyone say anything bad about the man."

You've read those things already. And you'll read them some more.

Earlier in this chapter, McClurg, the Board of Regents chairman, called Osborne a "Nebraska and USA treasure." And that's what many others have said, in different ways.

"Great leaders are innovative," McClurg said. "Under Tom's leadership, UNL has been first in building student-athlete support programs in strength training, academic support, life skills develop-ment, nutrition, and head-injury detection and treatment research. He has always led with a primary focus on the support of the student-athlete, and much of his success is measured in the successful lives of student-athletes – lives well lived, fulfilling their capability."

During the news conference at which Osborne announced his schedule for retiring, Chancellor Perlman referred to "the pride that Nebraskans have for not only winning and losing but for the holistic view that we take for student-athletes, that life skills are important, that academic success is important. That these students are going to be out as adults and as part of the athletic department's goal, just like in the university, are real roles to train them to be successful," he said.

"So I think that's a commitment. I think engagement of the fans, fans play an important role here. Former student-athletes play an important role here, and I think you have to be open and embracing of all the constituents of athletics."

He was talking about athletic department considerations in identifying Osborne's successor, considerations that reflected Osborne's concerns long before he became athletic director.

Among Osborne's accomplishments as athletic director was the completion of the $8.7 million Student Life Complex on the west side of Memorial Stadium, 50,000 square feet devoted to the betterment of Husker student-athletes.

"Every university department should be focused on competing at the very top level, graduating students, being compliant with the rules, and respecting and supporting the student," McClurg said. "UNL's athletics department with Tom at the helm has performed on these goals at the highest level. These examples, consistently achieved over decades, resonate with Nebraskans and sports fans everywhere and are a working definition of leadership."

This chapter began with Rimington, the two-time All-American and Academic All-American, no better embodiment of the term student-athlete.

"Thinking back on what made Coach Osborne such a good leader, I think integrity was the cornerstone quality," said Rimington, president of the Boomer Esiason Foundation. "We followed Coach because we trusted him. He was always consistent and competent.

"He spread the credit for our successes and took the blame for our failures. He was dedicated to bringing the best out of the players on the field and in the classroom. His support of our tremendous strength training and academic facilities were instrumental in getting the very best out of his players. When his players stumbled and didn't fulfill their obligations, he held his players accountable in a stern but fair way."

Osborne was creative on the football field, as his trick plays illustrate. But he also was creative off the field, "with the implementation of the Unity Council, where team policies and discipline were determined in large part by a trusted group of team leaders," Rimington said.

Osborne's vision was manifest in many ways.

Chapter Five:

PEOPLE SKILLS: WORKING AS A TEAM

"We all learned a lot from Coach Osborne if we were paying attention."

—JON HESSE, Husker linebacker (1994-96)

The elevator from the first floor to the second, where the football offices were located back then, included three or four players, all veterans except one, a freshman walk-on from a small Nebraska town. Tom Osborne joined them just as the No. 2 button was pushed, closing the doors.

Osborne acknowledged each of the players in turn, joking with one of the veterans about the thick gold chains he was wearing. "Got enough gold there?" he said. The others laughed.

Much to the surprise of the veterans, who certainly couldn't have done it, Osborne addressed the freshman walk-on by name, as well. Osborne also noted that he had read where the freshman's high school team had defeated its rival the previous weekend.

"He made the kid feel like a million bucks," Jon Hesse said several years later.

Hesse was among the veteran players on the elevator that day.

Osborne cared about his players, all of them. He cared about his assistant coaches. He cared about athletic department support personnel, from those in administration to those in maintenance. In short, he cared about people, and still does. People skills are integral to his leadership.

He'll acknowledge that, as he acknowledged the freshman on the elevator. But he'll do so only if prompted. Humility precludes taking credit for something he takes for granted. He treats people as he does because that's how they should be treated, with respect. And he receives respect in return.

"It was important that we performed well as a team and be successful on the field," said Osborne. "However, I wanted our players to do well in their lives off the field. I cared as much about a fourth-team player as I did about one of our starters. After practice, I'd spend time in the weight room with the players. I'd do some lifting and have conversations with guys. Over the course of the season, I'd have several conversations with all the players, and it was always their turf.

"I'd never talk about football. I'd ask about their families, their school work, how their high school team was doing, stuff like that. As a coach, you're never quite sure how you're coming across. But it's nice to know that your players still remember their personal chats many years later."

Players remember because the interest was genuine, not calculated, not simply a means to an end.

Steve McWhirter was a high school All-American from Fairfield, Iowa, talented enough that he earned a letter as a linebacker as a redshirted freshman in 1979. The NCAA lifted restrictions on redshirting freshmen the previous year, when he enrolled. He was among five Nebraska held out.

What made Osborne a "great leader is that I honestly felt that he truly cared about each and every player on the team," said McWhirter. "You might go several days without ever speaking to him. But you knew he cared about you in a deeper way than just if you were a star player."

McWhirter might well have become a star player. He had the credentials. And he did earn four letters, a rarity at the time, despite a knee injury. He was a starter as a senior and had one of his best days in his final game at Memorial Stadium, a 28-24 victory against rival Oklahoma in which he was credited with 14 tackles. But he battled injuries throughout his Husker career.

In the opener at Iowa his junior season, "I had a wide-open gap while blitzing, and the quarterback was in a drop-back pass," McWhirter said. "I was so surprised by the gap that I never 'broke down,' and the quarterback saw me at the last minute and made his move so I wouldn't hammer him."

As McWhirter planted to change direction, his left knee gave way with a ligament tear.

He knew immediately what had happened "because I had the same injury in my right knee a couple of years earlier," he said. Iowa upset the Huskers, adding insult to his injury.

The next week, as McWhirter was leaving the training room after some physical therapy for the injured knee, he encountered his position coach, who "pointed at me and said, 'God punished you for not breaking down and making that play,'" said McWhirter.

The assistant coach wasn't aware of Osborne, who was right behind him. "Coach 'O' got red in the face, which was when you knew he was serious, and let my position coach have it," McWhirter said. "He made it very clear that God didn't make that happen and wanted to make sure I didn't believe it. Now, I know that my position coach didn't mean it, but Coach 'O' knew what the injury probably meant for my season and how tough that was emotionally for me to deal with.

"At the time it really didn't make me feel better but later it stuck with me."

Because of the knee injury, McWhirter lost the starting job, though he did return later in the season. He underwent surgery on the knee following the season and missed all of spring practice his senior year. The next spring, after completing his eligibility, he went with Osborne to a Fellowship of Christian Athletes banquet in Wichita, Kansas. Osborne, the featured speaker, "thought they might want another speaker, so he asked me to go along," said McWhirter, who picks up the story there.

"Spring on the plains can bring some interesting weather, and that day was wicked," he said. "The plane was very small and to make a long story short, the ride was horrible. The plane was thrown all over. We lost radio contact and for a period of time, the dash gauges quit working.

"Coach 'O' was in the process of getting his flying license, so he sat up front with the pilot and I rode in the back. I just hung on to what I could, and frankly, got to the point that I knew we were going to die that day. To this day I hate to fly on any plane. Anyway, Coach 'O' saw what that ride did to me and he knew without asking how I really felt about getting back on that plane later that night.

"Spring is a very busy time for coaches, and the last thing he probably needed to do was to waste more time than necessary on this two-hour banquet in Kansas. But instead of putting me through another flight that night, he told me after the banquet that he thought we should rent a car and drive back to Lincoln. I was relieved like you can't believe and would have preferred to walk than fly. We spent most of the night driving back to Lincoln. That was before cellphones, and I can only imagine the work he kept thinking about that wasn't getting done. The point is I doubt very much that there is another head coach who would have done that, particularly for a player that was done playing."

McWhirter's story embodies Osborne's serving heart as well as his people skills, and both helped ensure that those who played for him would respond to his coaching and the principles it embodied.

"Every day, and I mean every day, Coach 'O' emphasized one thing over everything else and that was: You either get better or you go backwards," McWhirter said. "So what he tried to get us to believe in was giving our maximum effort every day, to do the things every day, and if we did that, the outcomes of the game in the fall would take care of themselves.

"We didn't lose very often, but when we did lose, he never beat us up if he felt as a team we prepared and played with maximum effort. I was there for five years in the program and he never wavered one day from emphasizing that belief."

McWhirter placed special emphasis on "never" in both sentences.

As McWhirter said, Nebraska didn't lose very often. The Huskers were a combined 41-8 with two Big Eight championships in his four seasons. If not for a loss at Penn State, mentioned elsewhere in this book, the 1982 Huskers almost certainly would have played for a national championship.

Jamie Williams and Roger Craig were also on those teams. Williams, like McWhirter, was among the five freshmen who redshirted in 1978, while Craig arrived in 1979 and didn't redshirt. Also, like McWhirter, Williams and Craig were from Iowa, high school teammates, in fact.

Williams has since returned. He's Nebraska's Associate Athletic Director of Diversity and Leadership Initiatives, a position that probably wouldn't surprise anyone who knew him as a Husker. "Tom was the only guy who really talked to me about academics and how I could get a degree," he has said of his recruitment out of Central High School in Davenport, Iowa.

As others say in this book, Osborne's interest in those he coached went well beyond the field.

Osborne had been Nebraska's head coach for only five years when he recruited Williams, a prep All-American in basketball as well as football. But he was already a presence, according to Williams. Snow was falling in Davenport when Osborne made a visit to the Williams home. Jamie looked out the window and saw Osborne standing in the accumulating snow: "That's the cat I've seen on TV."

Williams was a two-time All-Big Eight tight end at Nebraska and then played 12 seasons in the NFL. For four of those seasons he was a San Francisco 49ers co-captain. Before returning to Nebraska, he earned a master's degree at San Jose State and received a doctorate from the University of San Francisco. He's been a screenwriter, a corporate coach and an athletic director, establishing a Division II program with 16 sports at San Francisco's Academy of Art University.

Williams' doctorate is in leadership. "I've studied the topic and Tom Osborne," he said. "Tom was a consistent leader. Whatever he told you on Monday you could believe it on Friday. He didn't flip-flop like a fish out of water. With positive consistency like that, you are talking about integrity. A lot of want-to-be leaders flip-flop. You could count on Tom and believe him because he was so consistent."

A focus of this chapter is people skills, and Williams can attest to that aspect of Osborne's leadership as well. "Coach is the most 'angelic' of all the leaders I've been around," Williams said. "Angels arise during times of conflict and do their work in subtle ways, and then they are gone. With Tom, you didn't know how much he quietly worked on applied structure to your life and career.

"Later, you know and say, 'Wow.'"

As Osborne said earlier in this chapter, he tried to connect with his players in non-football ways. After he established himself as a player, Williams occasionally played tennis with his coach. "Of course, I let him beat me so I didn't get demoted," Williams has said. "But he was very comfortable with coaching me and then playing tennis with me. I thought that was cool." And so it was.

Tennis was another way in which Williams saw Osborne's competitiveness. "Tom's one of the most competitive people ever. He proved you didn't have to be loud and profane to be intensely competitive," said Williams. "Tom was the true-life general.

"He did many calculations before the engagement of conflict. He always connected all the dots and didn't rush into things with a lot of emotion. Tom Osborne is the pinnacle of great leaders. At 75, his wisdom is deeper now. As his motor has slowed down, his wisdom has gotten richer. He's now more of a peace-maker and teaches us that cooler minds always prevail."

Osborne was "genuine," Craig said, and accessible. "If a player had a problem, he'd find a way to solve it. As players, we could talk to him about anything. Coach had time for all of us and so many coaches don't." And again, that accessibility included fourth-string players as well as stars.

Craig, who inexplicably is not yet enshrined in the Pro Football Hall of Fame despite impressive numbers as well as three Super Bowl rings, was among the latter. "Roger Craig was a heck of a back, certainly one of the top three backs that I ever coached," Osborne said.

Craig played with the freshman team his first season at Nebraska. As a sophomore, he rushed for 769 yards, averaging 7.1 yards per carry, and 15 touchdowns – as the third-string I-back. Prior to his junior season in 1981, Osborne said Craig "has a chance to be the most complete running back we've had here." And Craig's performance supported that: 1,060 rushing yards, a 6.1-yards-per-carry average and six touchdowns. The rushing yardage was third-most in the Big Eight Conference. But why the dramatic drop-off in touchdowns? He shared time with sophomore Mike Rozier, who transferred after one season at Coffeyville (Kansas) Community College.

Rozier, of course, would win the Heisman Trophy in 1983, after becoming only the second college player to rush for 2,000 yards in a season.

If not for the presence of Rozier, Craig might well have been a serious Heisman Trophy candidate his senior season in 1982. Instead, he agreed to try playing fullback in order to get both him and Rozier on the field at the same time. "Coach Osborne asked me to move," Craig has said. "Mike and I traded off (in 1981). We never got in a rhythm, so would I move to fullback?'"

Osborne said the coaches had no intention of making "an average fullback out of a great I-back." The experiment didn't work. The point was moot to some degree, anyway, because Craig was hampered by injuries, first a thigh bruise that kept him off the travel roster for the Penn State game and then an ankle sprain. Even so, Craig never missed a practice that season.

Former Husker Trev Alberts, the Butkus Award winner as a senior in 1993, includes Craig among "guys that he (Osborne) really, really appreciated probably," not just because of their ability but also because they would "put the team above personal interest," said Alberts.

Osborne "just was not interested in selfish players," Alberts said.

Despite being limited his senior year, after alternating with Rozier as a junior and being third-string as a sophomore, Craig finished fourth on Nebraska's career-rushing list, and the San Francisco 49ers selected him in the second-round of the NFL draft. "I thought the 49ers drafted me because of my work ethic," Craig has said. And because of Osborne's recommendation.

Whatever the reasons, the wisdom of the 49ers' choice was quickly apparent. Even though he caught only 16 passes at Nebraska, he was a perfect fit for coach Bill Walsh's West Coast offense. Craig was the first running back in NFL history with 1,000 yards receiving and rushing in the same season. He rushed for 1,050 yards and had 1,016 receiving yards (on 92 catches) in 1985. He also led the league's running backs in receptions in six consecutive seasons during his 11-year NFL career.

"He's the ultimate in dedication and attitude," Walsh told *San Francisco Examiner* columnist Art Spander in October of 1985. "Right from the start he was willing to learn, and he's still learning. What a wonderful player. He plays as if he just appreciates the opportunity to be here."

Craig was a reflection of Osborne and his values, the focus of this book.

A story recounted by Spander illustrates Craig's character. The young daughter of a sports writer, who covered the Nebraska beat while Craig was a Husker, darted in front of a car in a residential neighborhood. She wasn't seriously injured, just shaken, as were her parents, who rushed her to the hospital as a precaution. Craig learned of the accident and sent the girl a note, wishing her well.

That Craig, whose brother Curtis preceded him at Nebraska, picked the Huskers out of high school was, in part, a result of Osborne's people skills. "He was a man of his word," said Craig.

His junior season – when Williams was a senior – Craig suffered a broken leg in the opening game and was sidelined the rest of the way. Recruiters who came to see Williams showed little interest in him. He was "worried about my future," Craig said. "Coach (Osborne) came to visit me and said, 'Roger, don't worry; we'll be back to get you next year.' The man lived up to everything he ever told me. He walked the talk better than anyone. Coach believed in me, and that's all I needed in my football career."

Years later, long after Craig had carried the ball for the last time in his No. 21 Husker jersey, Osborne would see him and ask about his family, including his younger sister – by name. "How's Rosiland?" Osborne would ask. "It's amazing. He's so great with names," said Craig.

"That's what I respect the most about him. People, to him, mean a lot."

Hesse's story at the beginning of this chapter illustrated that. "If every human was like Tom Osborne and had his goodness, the human species would be a couple of thousand years ahead," Hesse said.

That football is a violent game might seem a paradox. But "Coach taught us that you can be a nice guy and still hit people hard on the football field," said Hesse. "He was an extremely tough individual but had a tender heart. The Lawrence Phillips situation proves that."

The "Phillips situation," discussed elsewhere in this book, illustrated several aspects of Osborne's leadership, including his people skills. To dismiss Phillips from the team for his actions would have been justified. But it also would have taken away the one thing that might have been his salvation, football. So Osborne suspended him instead, a decision that drew considerable criticism.

"Coach was very sensitive to those kinds of scenarios," Hesse said. "College scholarships are really one-year contracts, but not at Nebraska. If you agreed to come play for Coach, he'd commit to you for four years so you could get your degree." Phillips didn't finish a degree, of course, or even make it through four years. But Osborne held up his end of the agreement, and then some.

As the Hesse quote leading into this chapter points out, those who paid attention learned a lot from Osborne and how he handled situations such as the one involving Phillips. "A deeply religious man, he just lived his life in the correct way," said Hesse. "Each year at training, he'd take a half-hour and speak to us about his relationship with God and how it helped him. He spoke about the choices he'd made in his life and the difference that had made. Then he walked the walk in front of us.

"He was never a micro-manager, and he taught all of us to have the courage of our convictions. It doesn't matter what other people think; you've got to be willing to go down on that ship."

As others have said in this book, Osborne maintained composure under the most trying circumstances. "I never saw Coach upset, even in a bad game," Hesse said. "His philosophy was that it's not what happens to you but how you react to what happens to you."

That's no surprise. Again, Osborne was a teacher, literally. At one point, he considered a job at Augustana College that would have combined teaching with being the head football coach. Until 1967, he divided his time at Nebraska teaching as well as coaching.

"Tom was a teacher at heart, and one of the lessons he always taught us was: You don't have to be fanatical and emotional to be successful," said Dr. Rand Schleusener. "His philosophy was that after about four plays, the emotion of the game will go away so now where are you? Coach emphasized preparation and consistency. Those two elements will always stand the test of time."

Schleusener, an orthopedic surgeon in Rapid City, South Dakota, started for two seasons at offensive guard for Osborne's Huskers and was a two-time, first-team Academic All-American. He carried the ball on the guard-around play, the "fumblerooski" described in an earlier chapter, running 15 yards for a touchdown against Oklahoma as a junior in 1979. He was a co-captain as a senior.

"Coach had our visible and available best interests in mind," Schleusener said. "Like a good military officer, he looked out for his troops because he valued us. There'd be 100 kids on the field, doing their stretching drills, and Coach would walk around, visiting with everyone out there. He'd talk to them personally about their lives or schoolwork or their family back home. Coach was aware of what we were doing because he cared about us and had our best interests at heart."

That's a consistent theme among those who played for Osborne.

"Coach had a really deep caring for anyone around him," said Craig Johnson. "He knew all the players by name on the first day of practice. He'd come up to me and say, 'Craig, how are you doing?' Stuff like that. That meant a lot to a freshman with all sorts of doubts about where he fit in."

Johnson and Schleusener were teammates. Johnson, a freshman in 1977 when Schleusener was redshirted, played running back, and though he was never a regular starter, he earned all-conference honorable mention as a senior, evidence of the depth at his position.

Johnson had remarkable success in three games against Kansas, scoring six touchdowns and rushing for over 400 yards. And he was good enough to make it to the final cut with the New England Patriots as a free agent following his career at Nebraska. He has his own real estate company in Omaha.

Osborne's work ethic "was second to no one's. He really put in the time. Also, his organizational skills were exceptional," Johnson said. "We were so well organized every day and that was reflected in our ability to get the most out of each player. The end result was success on the field.

"Coach truly believed in what he was doing."

Ralph Brown was a Husker freshman nearly 20 years later, in 1996, and Osborne's interaction with players was so much the same then that Johnson's words might just as well have been Brown's.

"My freshman year we had 180 guys out for the team," said Brown. "Coach knew the first and last names of every one of them. During the stretching drills, he'd go up and down the rows and talk to every player and use their names. He didn't have to do that, but he made it a point to know all his players personally. That's why we all loved him and played hard for him."

Brown played hard from the moment he stepped on campus. He played without redshirting and started every game at cornerback, 52 in a row, the second-most in NCAA history when he finished in 1999. He was the Big 12 Defensive Newcomer of the Year in 1996, a three-time, first-team All-Big 12 honoree and a consensus All-American as a senior. He also was a co-captain as a senior.

He set school records for pass break-ups in a game, season and career, and the teams on which he played had a combined record of 45-7, with a national championship, two Big 12 championships and three bowl victories. In addition, Brown had a degree in communication studies when he played his final game at Nebraska, a 31-21 victory against Tennessee in the 2000 Fiesta Bowl.

Osborne "was a fanatic on details with us, but he took care of the details of his life first. Then he infused and injected them into us every day," Brown said. "We respected him so much for that. I have tried to emulate Tom Osborne in my everyday life.

"He's one of the main reasons I am what I am today."

Brown, who played for 10 seasons in the NFL, owns B3ST Sports Training and B3ST Apparel Co.

Mike Fultz played five seasons in the NFL then returned to Lincoln, his home, to serve as an educator and coach. He was a member of Osborne's first recruiting class in 1973, coming from Lincoln High School, where he played fullback on offense. He was listed as a running back when he arrived at Nebraska, even though listed at 6-foot-4 and 230 pounds.

He was moved to defensive tackle and earned All-America recognition as a senior, as well as first-team all-conference honors for a second time.

Fultz saw Osborne as a young head coach. "Tom talked football with us," said Fultz. "But he spent a lot of time discussing life issues as well. He stressed the importance of education and finishing school. Along with that, he stressed the importance of family and having real friends in your life. Coach was respectful to his players. He didn't run around whooping and hollering.

"I never heard him cuss. The players liked him."

That was an aspect of Osborne the teacher, according to Neil Smith. "He trusted and believed in his assistants and his players," Smith said. "And we felt the same way about him. All of his players came from different parts of the country, and some had difficult backgrounds.

"But he taught us how to play in one accord while he was teaching us the value of life. In the process, I never heard him yell, scream or curse . . . ever."

The Huskers took a flier on Smith out of high school in New Orleans. They had one scholarship available – the 1984 class included only 17 players – and they offered it to him based on potential as much as anything. No other major colleges offered him, and only a few small colleges showed an interest, including Grambling, Florida A&M and Southern University.

Nebraska's interest in the 6-foot-5 Smith (he was listed at 6-6 as a Husker freshman), who played basketball as well as football at New Orleans' McDonogh 35 High School, was a result of having noticed him on film of another player at the school it was recruiting. Though Smith's dream was to play in the NFL, his chances didn't seem all that promising. He had the height certainly, but he was generously listed at 230 pounds on recruiting lists. The truth was he weighed closer to 200 pounds when he arrived at Nebraska. That was hardly heavy enough for the position he played, defensive tackle.

Smith started on the Husker junior varsity as a freshman then, after redshirting, was a back-up for two seasons. Nebraska's weight program, under the direction of Boyd Epley, helped transform him into an All-American and first-round NFL draft pick of the Kansas City Chiefs, the second player picked.

By his senior season, Smith weighed 260 pounds and had the nickname "Twisted Steel." He also could run the 40-yard dash in 4.63 seconds, electronically timed, making him the fastest defensive lineman in Husker history at the time.

Oh yes, he realized his NFL dream. He played 13 professional seasons and established himself among the top pass rushers in league history.

"Coach Osborne just wanted us to do our job," Smith said. "He believed in his system and in his players. We all had respect for him because we knew he loved his players and wanted the very best for all of us long after our football days were over. To this day, I know I could call Coach Osborne if I needed help, and he'd be there for me."

Broderick Thomas was Smith's teammate on Nebraska's Blackshirt defense, finishing a distinguished career as an outside linebacker in 1988, when he was a co-captain.

Thomas brought the nickname "Sandman" with him from Madison High School in Houston, Texas. His recruitment came down to the Huskers and Oklahoma; he wasn't interested in Texas. And Osborne was the difference, even though Thomas was inclined to go to Oklahoma when the recruiting process began. "When I went to Nebraska, Coach Osborne's reputation preceded him," said Thomas. "I had the sense I was in the presence of someone very important, who was going to help mold me and give me an opportunity to be a great young man."

Those in his neighborhood, as well as at his high school, also were impressed when Osborne visited, Thomas said, and the impression Osborne made on his mom was a significant factor in his decision to sign a letter of intent with the Huskers. She told him she knew she could trust Osborne.

"Coach is a very quiet person, but the way he carries himself allows him to speak very loud. He speaks in volumes," Thomas said. "What you see in Coach is exactly who he is. He delegates fame and fortune to those around him. The man is very humble, but he stands very tall."

Thomas was determined to play without redshirting, though Osborne promised only that he would have an opportunity to earn playing time. He did, playing in eight games as a freshman. He became a starter his sophomore year, earning first-team All-Big Eight honors for the first of three times. He was a first-team All-American as a junior and senior, when his selection was unanimous.

That he wasn't a unanimous All-American as a junior wounded the pride that drove him. "I was totally embarrassed, humiliated; that's what I was," he said at the time.

Even though he stood 6-foot-3 and weighed 250 pounds as a senior, Thomas was still among Nebraska's fastest defensive ends. His 40-yard dash time was 4.76 seconds, speed that contributed to his sacking quarterbacks 22½ times, among 39 tackles-for-loss, as a Husker. His determination was reflected in the fact that he played in two games his junior season with a lower-leg hairline fracture.

Thomas was a first-round NFL draft pick, the sixth player selected in 1989, and played 10 seasons in the NFL, the first five with the Tampa Bay Buccaneers, the last three with the Dallas Cowboys. He remains passionate about Nebraska and Osborne.

"Coach was a stickler about having his players prepared for anything that could come up in a game on Saturday," said Thomas. "He had all the i's dotted and the t's crossed. All the punctuation marks were in the right spots and the capital letters were all lined up properly. Coach would talk to us in a calm voice, with no ranting and raving. You'd have no questions unanswered because Coach was so clear about what he expected from you. I'm proud to tell the world that Tom Osborne was my coach."

Thomas was a member of a recruiting class ranked among the best in Osborne's 25 seasons, despite the fact that just a couple of weeks before letter-of-intent-signing day, the 47-year-old Osborne underwent coronary bypass surgery.

Though Osborne, a dedicated jogger, was physically fit, he had been experiencing a tightness in his chest for a month or two, and tests showed blockage in an artery. He chose the surgery over two other treatments. During the three-hour surgery, doctors bypassed two obstructions in a main artery.

Prior to the surgery, Osborne said one of his biggest concerns was how it would affect recruiting. For one thing, he wouldn't be on the road for 10 days at a critical time. For another, he wanted to assure those who had committed that he would be fine and coaching them. A week after the surgery, Osborne spoke at a news conference, answering questions about recruiting as well as his recovery. If things stayed as they were, Nebraska would have a "tremendous" recruiting class, he said.

Thomas was a reason for the 1985 recruiting class's high ranking, as was Steve Taylor, a quarterback from San Diego Lincoln High School, where he broke records held by Marcus Allen. Taylor and Thomas were roommates as Husker freshmen.

"Whatever Coach says he'll do . . . he'll do it," Taylor said. "When he recruited me, he said two things: 'You'll get a chance to play quarterback and you'll get a great education.' Other recruiters promised all sorts of things, but Coach lived up to his two promises."

Taylor, like Thomas, played enough to earn a letter as a true freshman, after starting four junior varsity games. Also like Thomas, he started for three seasons and was a co-captain in 1988. He earned All-America recognition as a junior and was a two-time, first-team All-Big Eight selection.

Taylor could run as well as pass. He held most of Nebraska's rushing records for quarterbacks when he finished his career. His play reflected the evolution of Osborne's offensive system, from one that was primarily passing to the option attack directed by Tommie Frazier and Scott Frost that produced the three national championships in Osborne's final four seasons.

"Coach was extremely loyal. He'd do all he could to give you a chance to succeed," said Taylor, who played briefly in the Canadian Football League before returning to Lincoln, where he has his own real estate business. "In fact, he'd give some guys a second and third chance."

Osborne is "the most consistent man I know, on and off the field," Taylor said.

Charlie McBride was the defensive coordinator when Thomas and Smith wore the black practice jerseys denoting Blackshirts. In fact, he was the coordinator for a majority of the defensive players quoted in this book. No other coach had more of an influence on Nebraska's

Blackshirt tradition than did McBride, who held the coordinator's title for the final 18 of his 23 seasons as a Husker assistant.

McBride had played against Nebraska at Colorado and was an assistant coach at Wisconsin when Osborne called. McBride had been at Wisconsin for seven years, the first five as an offensive line coach. The call came while he was attending the college coaches' annual convention in Miami, Florida, following the 1976 season. He was happy at Wisconsin, not necessarily looking for a different job.

Osborne was at the convention, looking to replace a pair of defensive assistants, Monte Kiffin and Warren Powers – both of them former Huskers, by the way. Kiffin was Nebraska's first assistant to have the title "defensive coordinator," getting it when Osborne succeeded Bob Devaney in 1973.

No assistants had coordinator titles under Devaney, though Kiffin oversaw the defense after George Kelly left for his alma mater, Notre Dame, following the 1968 season, while Osborne did the same for the offense. Kiffin also coached the defensive line, and Powers coached the defensive backs. Kiffin had left for Arkansas, Powers for Washington State, where he would be the head coach.

McBride has recounted his first contact with Osborne more than once. When Osborne called his room at the coaches convention, "I thought somebody was pulling my chain. 'No, really, who is this?'" I might have said that twice," McBride has said. "You know how Tom is. 'No, this is Coach Osborne.'"

As others in this book have pointed out, Osborne's reputation preceded him. McBride recalled that on the day after Thanksgiving in 1976, he and his wife Debbie watched Oklahoma defeat Nebraska 20-17, and during the telecast, he told her he'd like to work for "that guy" on the Husker sideline someday. That guy was Osborne. And McBride accepted the job as Nebraska's defensive line coach.

Osborne hired Lance Van Zandt from Kansas to be the Huskers' secondary coach and defensive coordinator, a title no Nebraska assistant held in 1981, after New Orleans Saints coach Bum Phillips hired Van Zandt to coach his secondary. Osborne "didn't like titles, period," McBride has said.

Even so, someone had to be responsible. Osborne was for the offense, serving as his own coordinator for all of his 25 seasons. And in 1982, he gave McBride the defensive coordinator's title. Under McBride, the Blackshirts ranked in the top 10 nationally in total defense 11 times and scoring defense 10 times. No defense was more dominant than McBride's last, which ranked second in passing defense, third in scoring defense, fourth in total defense and sixth in rushing defense. That he coordinated the 1999 defense was evidence of his loyalty to Osborne. He would have retired when Osborne stepped aside in 1997 but agreed to stay on and help Frank Solich in the transition.

"Tom was very patient with his players but didn't let you know it," said McBride. "Each player was part of the team, not just the first- or second-stringers. Many big-time coaches couldn't tell you the names of their third-team guys. Tom knew every one of his players and knew all of the parents as well. Tom was very hands-on. He was never a big-timer. He wanted to take part in all phases of his program."

In addition, "Tom built respect with all of his players," McBride said. "He never embarrassed a kid publicly and never used foul language. He never wore his religion on his sleeve but just lived out his faith. Tom never tried to change the make-up of his players but would steer them in the right direction. Tom never went back on his word. Whatever he promised he'd deliver.

"I never heard a negative word about him. Every player respected him."

Bryan Siebler, for example, a member of Osborne's 1982 recruiting class from Fremont, Nebraska, lettered three years and was a regular at safety the final two, sharing time as a junior and then starting as a senior. "Coach led by example and lived with integrity," Siebler said.

"He did things the right way and always maintained high moral and athletic standards. He wanted us to do our best on and off the field, and stressed our education because we couldn't play forever. Coach's main mission was for us to reach our potential by playing hard and tough."

Siebler was first-team academic all-conference as a senior in 1986.

"Coach Osborne had an enormous impact on my life," he said.

Grant Wistrom is among the most decorated defensive linemen in Husker history. A recounting of his accomplishments on and off the field could fill a chapter of its own. He was a two-time, first-team Academic All-American as well as a two-time, first-team, consensus All-American rush end. He was the Big 12 Defensive Player of the Year twice, the Big Eight Defensive Newcomer of the Year as a true freshman in 1994, and a three-time, first-team all-conference honoree.

Wistrom was the Big 12 Male Athlete of the Year for 1997-98, and he was an NCAA Top Eight Award winner. And he was inducted into the College Football Hall of Fame in 2009.

His pro football resume is similarly impressive. He was a first-round NFL draft pick, the sixth player selected in 1998 and played eight seasons with the St. Louis Rams and Seattle Seahawks. He has one Super Bowl ring, starting for the Rams in his second season, in Super Bowl XXXIV against the Tennessee Titans, and he played in Super Bowl XL, which the Seahawks lost to the Pittsburgh Steelers.

"Coach led by example," said Wistrom, who could have left Nebraska as a first-round NFL draft pick following his junior season but opted to return. "There were no artificial airs about him. He was the same behind closed doors as he was when in front of us as a squad. Whatever he portrayed to the world was exactly the same as when he and Mrs. Osborne were at home."

Wistrom's decision to stay at Nebraska is a tribute to Osborne's leadership as well as a reflection of Wistrom's character. He was determined to help Osborne win a third national championship after the Huskers came up short in 1996, following back-to-back titles in Wistrom's first two seasons.

Wistrom was a co-captain in 1997, along with Aaron Taylor, Vershan Jackson and Jason Peter, the other defensive co-captain. Wistrom and Peter, a tackle, led by force of will.

Peter's credentials were impressive as well, despite the fact he was playing with someone so decorated. He was a consensus All-American and a finalist for the Outland Trophy in 1997, when Taylor, his teammate, won the award as an offensive guard. Peter also was a two-time, first-team All-Big 12 selection and, like Wistrom, considered leaving Nebraska after his junior season.

"I'll never forget the honesty he showed us, and he wanted us to live that way as well," Peter said of Osborne. "It started in the recruiting process. Head coaches were streaming through my living room and promising my parents and me the world. Coach Osborne came for his visit and made no promises."

Osborne recruited Peter and his older brother Christian – also a defensive tackle and co-captain on the 1995 national championship team – out of Locust, New Jersey.

"He told me, 'I'll give you an opportunity to go to school and play football if you're good enough. The rest is up to you to take it from there.' As a 17-year-old youngster, that registered with me. Picking Nebraska was an easy decision for me to make," Jason Peter said. "There's just an honesty to the way Coach thinks and gets to a decision.

He looks at all sides of an issue, studies and analyzes the pros and cons and then goes ahead and makes the call. He's so honest; it may have hurt him as a politician."

Don Walton is a columnist and political writer for the *Lincoln* (Nebraska) *Journal Star* and has watched Osborne throughout his career. "I thought Tom was comfortable with public policy, but politics was not his game," said Walton. "It often rewards skills he never cared to practice or embrace, like attacking or diminishing an opponent, crafting policy positions to fit public opinion or for other political advantage, and focusing more on personal gain rather than teamwork or group goals.

"I think what we can learn from Tom's leadership skills is the value and strength of personal integrity and accountability, and the power of teamwork."

Those skills "are built on a foundation of integrity," Walton said. "People trust him and they respect him. He is direct and principled. He preaches and practices personal accountability and teamwork. He appears to be unflappable under pressure. I suspect he would credit much of his personal strength to his faith." More about that elsewhere in this book. Back to Jason Peter.

Like Wistrom, he also was a first-round NFL draft pick, the 14th player selected, by the Carolina Panthers. He played four seasons with the Panthers before injuries cut short his career.

As many players have, he dealt with some off-the-field issues in the NFL, which he recounted in a best-selling book, *Hero of the Underground*. "Now that I have kids of my own, I just hope they'll live life with the morals and values of Tom Osborne," he said. "If I could live my life with just half of his morals and values, I'd have lived a pretty good life. I've never heard anyone, including his players, say a bad word about the man.

"Coach has been a second father to thousands of kids and a first father to many who grew up without a father in the home."

Peter's words express several qualities of Osborne's leadership, including people skills, a focus of this chapter. "Coach was able to personalize his relationships with his assistants, his players and their families," said Keith Jones, another of the outstanding running backs (1984-87) who came to Nebraska from Omaha Central High School. He had the nickname "End Zone" and wore a No. 6 jersey, scoring 32 touchdowns during his Husker career. He was a two-time, first-team all-conference selection and still ranks in the top 20 on Nebraska's career-rushing list.

Osborne "got to know these people as real human beings, and as a result, his players responded to him," Jones said. "In 1984, I went to Nebraska for my recruiting visit. My uncle Steve went with me and met Coach Osborne. In 2004, I went back to Lincoln to be inducted into the Nebraska Hall of Fame. Coach hadn't seen Steve in 20 years. After acknowledging me, he said, 'Steve, how are you doing?' My uncle was floored by that gesture and still tells that story to this day. That put the icing on the cake for him. Tom Osborne took an interest in you and your family. You'd go to war for someone like that."

Enough said on Osborne's people skills and how they relate to his leadership, though this chapter could probably continue indefinitely.

Chapter Six:

A SERVING HEART: SERVANT LEADERS GAIN DEVOTED DISCIPLES

"Tom's faith is the rock that all this sits on."

—NANCY OSBORNE

The Nebraska football team was practicing in August of 1997, going through fall camp, two-a-day practices leading into what would be Tom Osborne's final season as head coach, though no one knew at that point he would be stepping aside. Details such as time and place really aren't important anyway, because what happened was repeated many times, in many ways, over 25 seasons.

It could have happened during Osborne's time in Congress, though in some other way, of course. It could have happened yesterday in the athletic department he now oversees – and will oversee until January 1, 2013, when he steps aside and spends the next seven months helping his successor, Shawn Eichorst, make the transition. Or it could happen tomorrow, again just in a different form. Football is simply the context, the frame of reference for the serving-heart principle.

In any case, the Huskers were running an offensive drill that day, a drill requiring defensive players as well, or at least stand-ins for defensive players. "Sometimes we use extra offensive players in there," assistant coach Ron Brown told a local newspaper reporter a day or two later. "Well, none of the extra offensive players or coaches jumped in at a linebacker's spot that was vacant."

So Osborne "jumped in there and did it," said Brown. "Normally, the head coach will say, 'You gotta get in there.' He saw that nobody had really picked up on it, so he just jumped in there and said, 'I'll play linebacker.' And he gave you the different read.

"It's just interesting to see coaches, head coaches, who could easily just point their finger at somebody and say, 'You do this. You do that,' the delegation principle, which I don't think is bad. I think it's important to have delegation. But he (Osborne) is the kind of man who, if there's slack in an area and he feels like it's going to be a stress for a player or an assistant coach, I've seen him so many times take on that so-called menial job on his own. That's an unusual trait for leaders in our society today."

Brown's words of 15 years ago hold firm today. They're as true in describing Osborne the athletic director as they were in describing Osborne the Hall of Fame coach. "Coach has always been consistent as a man of humility and servanthood," Brown said. "He understands the biblical command that to be the greatest of all, we need to be the servant of all. As Nebraska kept growing as a big-time football program, Tom kept reducing his own ego. In recruiting many of his players, Coach looked beyond the physical appearance and into the inner. I think that was because of his servant mentality."

Brown coaches Nebraska's running backs now. He coached the wide receivers and tight ends for 11 years under Osborne and continued for six years under Frank Solich. He was out of coaching the four years Bill Callahan was Husker head coach, during which time he served as state director of the Fellowship of Christian Athletes for Nebraska. Then Bo Pelini brought him back as tight ends coach in 2008.

Brown came to Nebraska from Brown University, his alma mater. He coached the defensive backs at Brown for three seasons, after one season as head freshman coach. He has a master's degree in public health from Columbia University. And he is vocal in his Christian faith, a man of clearly defined and deeply held principles, like Osborne. He is the author of several books on Christian character, and he and former Husker Stan Parker are co-founders of Mission Nebraska, a statewide Christian ministry.

When Nebraska traveled to Penn State in 2011, and the storm of controversy there made the game insignificant, Brown, who was elected to the FCA Hall of Champions in October of 2012, was asked to lead both teams in prayer on the field before the opening kickoff. His selection for such a responsibility came as no surprise to Cornhusker fans. But it was "not so obvious to me," Brown said with characteristic humility two days later. "I look in the mirror every day and I know what's in my heart and I know that I'm not always faithful to God like I should be."

You would be hard-pressed to find a former player or assistant who would say anything negative about Osborne, as this book illustrates. These are but a sampling of those who can offer insight into the man affectionately known as "Dr. Tom." And each in his or her own way is articulate in offering such insight, none more so than Brown, whose enthusiasm and energy are legend.

First and foremost, Osborne is a "gentleman," said Brown. "When I came here on my interview, he was opening doors for me. He carried my luggage at the airport. He picked me up, personally, at the airport, which doesn't happen all the time when you go on an interview."

Osborne had been Nebraska's head coach for 14 years when he contacted Brown about replacing Gene Huey, who had left to coach at Arizona State. The Huskers had a combined record of 53-9 the previous five seasons and had been ranked in the top five in the final Associated Press poll in all but one of those seasons. So Osborne's "reputation obviously had preceded him with me, even though I was from the East Coast, because I knew he was one of the more famous coaches in the country," Brown said. Also, "I heard about the kind of man he was, and I saw it in action."

That was immediately apparent from "just general conversation" on the telephone, Brown said. "Initial impression? Gentleman, very much a gentleman, very soft-spoken, very patient. He really listened. Sometimes, people tend to go on a monologue, maybe. A lot of people want to just cut a person off and say, 'It's time for me to talk.' He just kind of lets it go on and lets it go on. And then when there's a break in the action, he slips something in. I just noticed little things like that about him.

"He does the little things. It's not phony things. It's not like, 'Well, let me do these little things here, just to impress this guy and then once I hire him, I'll go back to my old, rotten ways.' He really is not on an ego trip, in any way. I think he sees himself as a servant, and in this day and age, that's kind of a bad word. People are offended by that word. But it's really a very important word that you don't see enough of today, particularly from people who are in high leadership positions. And I think that's probably what separates Tom from so many people. He is polite. He is genuine. He is a thank-you person."

That Osborne is a "thank-you person" inspires loyalty. "The natural tendency would be to take advantage of a person like that," Brown said. "But what happens after a while is, when someone serves you over and over again, there's a built-in human capacity to develop loyalty to that person. It's not just a one-way street. A lot of times when you're talking about loyalty, people are expecting it from the top to the bottom, 'You be loyal to me,' if you're the top guy."

Osborne's players and assistant coaches saw that it went both ways, however, that "this guy is loyal to me," said Brown. "Consequently, it's an incentive for me to be loyal to him. You would like to think there's an unconditional love and an unconditional loyalty, that no matter how bad someone treats you, you'll still, because of the greater cause, be loyal. But that's not normal human tendency.

"Tom, I think, has fostered over the years a loyalty around here because he has been loyal; he has demonstrated loyalty. And you know, he has really tried to emphasize the positive aspects of human character. In a game, a rival situation, you don't hate them . . . you don't learn how to hate them. You learn how to respect them. In fact, you learn how to respect them so much it brings more out of you."

As a coach and now as athletic director, as well as when he was in Congress, Osborne has a plan. "He's on a mission, and when you're on a mission, you really learn how to budget your time," Brown said while Osborne was still coaching. "Part of his mission is out-reach and compassion. That's a big part of Tom's mission . . . and role-modeling, exampling. So I think he plans that kind of thing. I don't know that it's just a spontaneous thing. It seems to me that he's the kind of guy who gets up early and does a good job before he goes to bed, planning what he's going to do tomorrow. He just doesn't live off the seat of his pants. There's a rhyme and reason to what he does."

Nothing has changed. Brown could just as easily have said those things yesterday instead of 15 years ago, when Osborne was considering stepping aside from coaching. And he will say the same things tomorrow. Osborne's consistency of character, his consistency in principles, won't change.

That Osborne is a gentleman should not be construed as lacking competitiveness. No coach earned a place in the Hall of Fame with passivity. As a coach he was a "tremendous competitor. That soft-spoken, mild-mannered-Clark-Kent, outward persona can't be mistaken for the fact that he does step into the phone booth before practice and before a game and puts on the Superman outfit," Brown said. "It's inside. He is one of the best competitors you'll ever see, a feisty competitor as a matter of fact."

In many ways, Osborne was the definitive coach for Nebraska, and not only because he is a Nebraskan. He embodies many of the qualities Nebraskans see in themselves, or would hope to see in themselves, anyway. "He's very diligent," Brown said. "And I don't know that there's any magical thing about him other than he's a hard-working guy and he's diligent. He's on a mission."

That mission wasn't complete when Osborne left coaching. And it won't be complete when he steps aside as athletic director. It will continue in many ways, including the TeamMates program he and wife Nancy started. That program is discussed later in this book.

Brown described Osborne as a "thank-you" person, and Bill Doleman offers an illustration. Doleman was host to Osborne's statewide, hour-long, highlights show on Nebraska Educational Television in the mid-1990s. The show "took a lot of hard work by a lot of people to get it on the air each week," said Doleman. "At the end of the season Tom would go around and ask each person, including a large (university) student staff, what their job was. Then he'd write a personal bonus check for each person. That was just his way of saying 'thank you.' He looked out for everybody."

Doleman worked in the Nebraska sports information office during his sophomore year at the university. "I went from a fan to working on the inside," he said. "I started to see quite quickly that the personality of Tom Osborne set the tone for the whole place.

"There was a respect and reverence for Tom from everyone. He'd walk through the training table area, and the swimmers and gymnasts would look up and whisper, 'It's Coach Osborne.' That reverence came from the way he treated everyone in the athletic department and beyond.

"He was so consistent in who he was, and that was the result of his consistency in his integrity and convictions. Tom was the same on the outside of the program at Nebraska as he was on the inside, and that was not made up. It is his consistency as a man and the way he treats people that sets Tom apart. I've never been disappointed by Coach Osborne."

Doleman's experience in the sports information office, as well as six years doing the Osborne show and writing scripts for HuskerVision's highlight videos, provided him with unique opportunities to see how those who played for Osborne felt about their coach. In the aftermath of Osborne's handling of Lawrence Phillips "there were still a lot of national rumblings going on," Doleman said.

"The leaders of the team called a players-only meeting. I was standing nearby as the players filed into the room and shut the door. I could hear some loud voices as some of the guys went back and forth. Finally, I heard one loud voice say, 'We are not going to be the team to let this man down.' Those guys did not want Tom Osborne's reputation to be sullied. The leaders wanted everyone on the same page to protect their coach. It showed a lot of respect and love for the man.

"It was a very powerful moment in Nebraska football history."

Another very powerful moment in Nebraska football history was the Huskers' 24-17 victory against Miami in the 1995 Orange Bowl game, providing Osborne with his first national championship. Trev Alberts, a unanimous All-America outside linebacker, Butkus Award winner and Academic All-American who had completed his eligibility the previous season, was at the game and visited the Husker locker room afterward to congratulate his former coach.

When he entered the locker room, "you see his demeanor change," Alberts said during an interview a few years later, "and he says, 'Trev, I really feel bad you didn't get to win one of these.'"

The previous year, also in the Orange Bowl against Florida State, Alberts and the Huskers had come within a field goal at the end of winning a national championship.

"He genuinely cared about his players," said Alberts. "It wasn't fake. You can't act that kind of stuff. He was real about it. He cared about you. He wished that you got to participate. I believe coaching for him was more about seeing us succeed, almost like having kids."

Bill Bobbora was among those "kids," playing for Osborne in the late 1980s. He was recruited out of Amarillo, Texas, where he played defensive line in high school. But he made the transition to the offensive line at Nebraska and was the starting right guard as a senior in 1989.

"Coach truly embraced the concept of servant leadership, and he tried to instill it in all of us as fathers and business leaders," said Bobbora, who earned an MBA at the University of Texas in Austin and is now Senior Vice President of Cadence Bank in Houston. "We were too young to truly get it, but it was there. The culture he created at Nebraska was a family structure. We felt comfortable and secure, but we had very high goals and expected to do well. However it was not about wins and losses with Coach.

"He was more concerned about your effort and preparation and how you carried yourself on the field and in life. If you did that, Coach believed the wins would come as a result. He wanted a winning perspective in life for all of us."

Bobbora earned three letters on teams with a combined record of 31-6. And those teams won the right way. "Coach had a wonderful way of building confidence," said Bobbora. "For example, he'd say, 'Now, fellas, after you knock your man down, make sure you pick him up.'

"He made you feel you were better than you were."

Bobbora had insight into Osborne before he ever enrolled at Nebraska. As he was leaving a school that had offered him a scholarship following a recruiting visit, an assistant at the school with Nebraska connections, told him it appeared his decision had been made. "Tom Osborne's a fine man," the assistant said. "You're not going to find a better human, a better man in the world. I think you made up your mind a long time ago, where you needed to be, and I think it's with Tom Osborne."

Though his first choice going into the recruiting process was Notre Dame – Bobbora moved from Chicago to Amarillo in high school – the assistant had been right. "Coach constantly led by example," Bobbora said. "He wanted us to get good grades, be a gentleman. He built that into our culture and that put a high level of achievement that we put on ourselves."

John Parrella lined up against Bobbora during practice on the scout team in 1989. Bobbora was a starting offensive guard that season, remember, and Parrella was a redshirted sophomore defensive tackle. A two-time all-state honoree at Grand Island (Nebraska) Central Catholic High School, he had paid his own way and walked on at Nebraska the previous fall, after signing a letter of intent with Colorado. But the

Buffaloes pulled the scholarship before he enrolled, after other schools, including Nebraska, had reached their limits.

Parrella played tight end as a freshman. He was a starter at that position on the Husker junior varsity team. The move to defensive tackle took some time. He saw only limited action there in his third season. In the end, however, Colorado's loss proved to be the Huskers' gain. Parrella was put on scholarship and started for two seasons, earning All-Big Eight honors as a senior and serving as a co-captain.

"Everything he taught us he lived it himself," Parrella said of Osborne. "When he told us one thing he wanted from us, he did the exact same thing. You can't be a leader and live a different life."

Parrella went on to play 12 seasons in the NFL with the Buffalo Bills, San Diego Chargers and Oakland Raiders. He's now the football coach at Valley Christian High School in Dublin, California.

"To this day I can't call him Tom. It's always Coach Osborne," said Parrella. "He genuinely cared for his players and still does today. Not long ago I saw Coach and said, 'Thanks for your faith in Christ. It changed my life.' Now I'm serving the ultimate leader because of the life of Tom Osborne."

Osborne was a "selfless leader," said Barney Cotton, who played for him in the late 1970s and is now the offensive line coach and associate head coach under Bo Pelini. "First of all, I think he was an easy guy to follow because he was honest. He had integrity, which led to you respecting him. He was really smart, and he was a good communicator. And I think he treated people fairly. He wasn't a dictator. He was a guy that if he said, 'Hey, do it this way, I think it's going to work; I've got some experience doing it, follow me,' you had a tendency to follow him because he had those core values."

Also because of those core values, players didn't want to let him down. "I wanted him to look at me and be able to say, 'Hey, Coach, you can depend on me,'" Cotton said.

Osborne could do that, certainly. Cotton, who came from Omaha Burke High School, played a different position in each of his seasons at Nebraska. He was a starting offensive tackle on the junior varsity team as a freshman, an alternate center as a sophomore, a starting defensive tackle as a junior and a starting offensive guard as a senior, when he earned second-team All-Big Eight honors.

Wherever he was needed, that's where he played. Osborne was a "tireless worker," said Cotton. "He treated people with respect. He built up a trusting relationship and when he asked you to do something, you had an idea it might be in your best interests to try it. Within that, you kind of had a bunch of guys that bonded together. Then you've got a group of guys that are believing in the same thing and they start going in the same direction. I think it kind of builds momentum and his culture.

"I think that's what his culture was."

Cotton, who played three seasons in the NFL before a knee injury cut short his career, began coaching as a graduate assistant at Nebraska in 1987 and 1988, working with the freshman-junior varsity. His first full-time job was as offensive coordinator and offensive line coach at St. Cloud State. He was the head coach at Hastings (Nebraska) College for two seasons and assistant head coach, offensive line coach and offensive coordinator at New Mexico State for six years before becoming the offensive coordinator and offensive line coach at his alma mater in a staff restructuring in 2003.

A year later coach Frank Solich and his staff were replaced, and Cotton went to Iowa State as offensive coordinator and offensive line coach. He returned to Nebraska in 2008.

The point is, Cotton has seen many types of leadership at various levels, providing him a means of evaluating Osborne's unique leadership qualities.

"He wasn't a yeller and a screamer," Cotton said. "He was more of a soft communicator. I think he was a good teacher. He didn't motivate guys to play hard by intimidating them or anything like that. I don't know; he was just kind of a unique individual that people followed because he built a trusting and respectful relationship with them. And he got people to buy into chasing a common goal."

That he was a "soft communicator" didn't diminish his competitiveness. "We all knew how competitive he was," said Cotton. "I'm sure that some people didn't understand how this guy who was fairly dry, with kind of a dry sense of humor and kind of a soft-spoken guy . . . how does he coach a bunch of guys to play like crazed banshees?"

Sense of humor, dry or otherwise? Osborne, the stoic leader?

"Oh, he's funny as all dickens," Cotton said. "I don't want to say it's like a dry English humor. But he's funny. He's kind of licking his lips and sticking his tongue in his cheek. Things just kind of roll out. The punch line is kind of unexpected sometimes, but it's funny.

"You've got to pay attention or you might miss it."

As with so many of what he considers Osborne's qualities as a leader, Cotton understands them more as he coaches. The sense of humor, for example, "I saw it some" as a player, he said.

But he really saw it "as I got older and became a GA, late 20s or something like that, when you get to sit in on private coaches' meetings. Public speaking, he's going to tell jokes. But you could see that there was more to him because you were behind the scenes," said Cotton.

In addition to his own skills as a leader, Osborne "also was smart enough to surround himself with coaches with different personalities. There weren't nine guys that were just like him. I think that's the mark of a good leader; don't surround yourself with people just like you," Cotton said.

"There are different types of leadership styles."

Staff stability was another element of Osborne's coaching success. During his 25 years as head coach, he had only 26 full-time assistants, 12 of whom were with him for 10 years or more and six who were with him for at least 15 years.

Osborne retained assistant coaches because he allowed them to coach.

"I learned a lot about delegating from Bob Devaney; he did it very well," Osborne said. "He was not a micro-manager who'd jump into a drill and embarrass or belittle the assistant coach in charge. I learned it was important to take an assistant aside and talk privately. The old adage is true: Praise in public and criticize in private. As a head coach, I learned I couldn't control everything."

So he involved his assistants in the decision-making.

"My assistants were with me a long time, and we had very little turnover," he said. "Their jobs were clearly delineated, and I let them operate with very little interference. In our staff meetings, I encouraged new ideas. If you put people's ideas down, pretty soon you won't get any new ones. I wanted our meetings to be a forum for good, new ideas and input."

George Darlington was an Osborne assistant for all 25 years. He was the second assistant Osborne hired after succeeding Devaney, and he remained on staff until Solich restructured in 2003.

"Tom genuinely cared about people. The fourth-team guy was as important to him as a star player," said Darlington. "Then he had the capacity to follow up with people and not just once. He'd stay with it as long as necessary. Tom is extremely bright, and his competitive drive is much greater than people realized. He's always been tremendously driven."

He's also "a man of tremendous consistency, regardless of the circumstances," Darlington said. "His level of emotion was the same all the time, regardless of wins or losses."

Gene Huey was on Osborne's staff for 10 years, working with the split ends, wingbacks and tight ends. After stops at Arizona State (1987) and Ohio State (1988-91), he coached the Indianapolis Colts' running backs for 19 seasons (1992-2010).

Osborne was "very well-organized, leaving nothing left unturned in his preparation. He was very detail-oriented and on top of everything," said Huey. "When Tom took over for Bob Devaney, there were a lot of older guys on the staff. Tom retained them, which gave us a lot of stability and served as the foundation for a great deal of success at Nebraska. Many wives on our staff worked on the campus, some in the ticket office. That helped create a real family atmosphere."

Osborne "was an educator and teacher as much as he was a football coach. He was teaching his players life lessons as much as anything. Tom's faith gave him a strong foundation in life, which provided an inner peace and confidence that his beliefs were rock-solid. Under duress this allowed him to stay the course. It also gave him great wisdom and foresight as he made important decisions.

"Leadership lends itself to loneliness, and Tom's wife Nancy gave him strong support during those lonely times. She was instrumental in his success."

Nancy Osborne has the same consistency of character and serving heart as her husband.

"Tom is very intelligent and has the ability to assess a situation quickly without getting overly involved emotionally," she said. "This allows him to look at things clearly and objectively. As the athletic director, Tom wants what's best for the department and not for himself. He has the ability to balance all that as he thinks, 'What do we have to do to make the athletic department the best we can with the resources we have to work with?'

"Tom is very much the leader in our family, and he leads the same way as he does elsewhere. He has goals for our time and involvement with the grandkids and wants to do what's most beneficial for them. Tom's able to do this without usurping the guys of their roles of being the dads."

Osborne's unexpected retirement from coaching at age 60 was a result of many factors, including family. "My family has been very supportive, and, I think, has paid a pretty good price for me being allowed to do what I've done," he said at the news conference to announce he would be stepping aside after the 1998 Orange Bowl against Tennessee – and quarterback Peyton Manning. "I really appreciate Nancy's stance in all of this. She raised three children fairly single-handedly, and I don't think I've realized until recent years, maybe, how difficult some of that was."

The same could be said of their children: Mike, Ann and Suzi.

"I think sometimes being the head coach's children has some plusses," Osborne said. It also "has a lot of minuses. Certainly, my family has been very important to me. I don't know that you ever make up for the lost time, that you ever really, completely do that."

Like his dad, Mike Osborne played football at Hastings College. And like his dad, he was a quarterback. "My father leads with the heart of a servant," Mike Osborne said. "If a leader is willing to be a servant, that inspires the best in others. Dad has never tried to promote himself to have the fanciest title or have the biggest salary. He always has a group goal in mind.

"So he'll work the longest and the hardest to achieve those results. Dad doesn't need to scream and yell at you to get you motivated. He motivates others by his servant-hearted leadership approach."

Suzanne Hince, the youngest of the children, echoes her brother.

"My dad is a true servant leader," she said. "He has the ability to be non-judgmental. He gets to the facts and is very fair with everybody. His faith is a big part of how he leads."

It infuses all aspects of his life. "Tom has a humble attitude and doesn't need a lot of attention," Nancy Osborne said of her husband. "In fact, he'd rather not have the attention and be off fishing somewhere. Tom's faith is the rock that all this sits on."

Jeff Jamrog is among those who walked on, earned a scholarship, and played for Osborne. He was a three-year letterman at defensive end, a starter as a senior in 1987, when he earned first-team Academic All-America honors and an NCAA post-graduate scholarship.

He began a coaching career as a graduate assistant at Nebraska for two years, with stops as an assistant at South Dakota, Nebraska-Omaha and New Mexico State before returning to Nebraska in 2000 to coach the defensive line under Solich. When Solich and staff were let go following the 2003 season, Jamrog became the head coach at Minnesota State. Pelini brought him back in 2008.

Jamrog is the associate athletic director for football operations, among other things coordinating the walk-on program, and a member of Osborne's Nebraska Athletics Executive Team.

"Tom is a true servant leader who cares about others above himself," said Jamrog. "As the athletic director who oversees a multitude of sports, coaches and student-athletes, Tom knows that every decision he makes has to be in the best interest of Nebraska sports programs. As he serves others, he must frequently ask this question: 'What is the right thing to do?'"

Pat Logsdon is an associate athletic director and the Senior Women's Administrator as well as part of the Nebraska Athletics Executive Team. She worked in the football office when Osborne was head coach.

"Coach Osborne is a great leader because he possesses an uncanny ability to get others to willingly follow him as they aspire to do their very best for him," Logsdon said. "He leads with character, integrity, and values and is a great listener. He establishes a clear vision and is remarkable at creating a positive culture in which each person is treated with dignity and respect and feels valued. Coach Osborne has had such a profound influence on my life, as he has lived, as we all should aspire to live. I have never met a more dedicated, compassionate, trustworthy, ethical, and humble human being."

Doak Ostergard also is part of Nebraska's Athletics Executive Team as outreach director for football, a position Osborne created when he was hired as athletic director to ensure that former Huskers felt welcome around the program, something that wasn't the case under the previous administration. Osborne "recognized that everyone on the team had value and tried to maximize their contribution, no matter how small," said Ostergard, a football trainer during Osborne's tenure as coach.

"Plus, every relationship he had and has, was and is based on respect, so no matter how you felt about him or something that he has done, you had to respect him."

Mike Arthur is the director of strength and conditioning for the athletic department. He was on Boyd Epley's staff when Osborne was head coach. As related elsewhere, the strength and conditioning program became state of the art under Osborne, with Epley as the driving force. Many of Epley's assistants have gone onto success in the field of strength and conditioning, including Arthur.

"I've worked with coaches who worked out of a sense of fear, and they end up micro-managing everything so they can be in total control. Tom never did that. He empowered all of his staff members so they could do their best and work with a sense of freedom," Arthur said.

"Tom was never worried about the amount of money he was making. He was never afraid of injuries because he considered that just part of the game. I never saw him angry, especially in front of the players. As a result, his athletes were not afraid of making mistakes. Tom didn't try to build confidence as much as undoing the doubt and fear that plagues players. He wanted to leave an empty space for confidence to fill in.

"I have two favorite Tom Osborne quotes that stick with me to this day. One is: 'Things are going to change – they're either going to get better or get worse.' The other is: 'It's not about time-management. It's about self-management.'"

Bill Bennett saw Osborne as a young head coach as assistant sports information director. He later worked in sports information at UCLA. "Tom Osborne was a complete coach and person," said Bennett. "He was so much like John Wooden: intelligence, attention to detail and treating people with respect. Back in 1973 and '74, I didn't realize what a unique leader Tom was. But now it's all clear to me.

"How fortunate I have been to be around Tom Osborne and John Wooden."

Wooden and Dean Smith, another Hall of Fame basketball coach to whom Malcolm Moran compared Osborne in another chapter are prestigious company. Bobby Bowden can be added, as well.

An entire chapter could probably be devoted to the friendship between Bowden and Osborne, which had its roots in a four-game series between Florida State and Nebraska in the early 1980s. Interestingly enough, all four games were played in Lincoln, with the teams each winning two.

More about that follows. But first, something about Bowden, even though the Hall of Fame football coach doesn't really need an introduction. In fact, his leadership principles are presented in the second book of this leadership series, written with Rob Wilson and published in 2011.

Bowden is the second-winningest football coach in major college history, coaching Florida State to 300-plus victories, two national championships and 12 Atlantic Coast Conference titles. His teams there finished in the top five in the nation in 14 consecutive seasons and played in 28 consecutive bowls.

Bowden's first national championship came at Osborne's expense, when Florida State defeated the Huskers 18-16 in the 1994 Orange Bowl game – the fourth bowl in which the two coached against each other: the previous year's Orange Bowl and two Fiesta Bowls in the late 1980s. The Seminoles won all four of the bowl games, motivation for some of the changes at Nebraska that produced the three national championships in Osborne's final four seasons as coach.

Florida State won the first meeting in 1980, upsetting the No. 3-ranked Huskers 18-14. The week after the game, Bowden wrote an open letter complimenting Nebraska and its fans.

"I have never seen people with more class than I saw at Nebraska last week," he wrote in the letter, published in Nebraska newspapers. "The Nebraska fans, players, cheerleaders, band, officials, coaches, etc., gave me a living testimony of what college football should be all about."

That class was a reflection of the Huskers' head coach, Osborne.

"I remember when we played out there in 1980 and beat Nebraska, which doesn't happen very often," Bowden said, recalling that game. "As we walked off the field, the Nebraska fans stood up and clapped for us. I can't say enough good things about Tom Osborne and the University of Nebraska. The Nebraska athletic department was so kind to visiting teams and a lot of that can be credited to Tom.

"He was a great organizer, first of all, and a strong Christian. He didn't flaunt it, but you knew it was there."

Bowden also is a strong and active Christian, of course. In 2004, the Fellowship of Christian Athletes established the National Bobby Bowden Award in his honor, and he has been presented the Children's Champion Award for Leadership Development by the Children's Hunger Fund through his FCA association. Among his "Leadership Insights," included on the back cover of *Bobby Bowden on Leadership*, is: "There is no substitute for faith in God." Osborne would echo that.

Osborne's first FCA experience was at the second-ever FCA conference in Estes Park, Colorado, the summer between his sophomore and junior years at Hastings College, attended by such recognizable athletes as Doak Walker, Otto Graham, Bob Richards and Don Meredith, then a collegian at SMU.

"The Estes Park experience was particularly important to me because I sensed a virility and vitality about Christianity – as well as a sense of warmth, a sense of acceptance and love," Osborne wrote in his first book, *More Than Winning*, with John E. Roberts, published in 1985.

Osborne recounts how he returned to Hastings College and tried, unsuccessfully, to set up a Bible study group. "I don't see any incompatibility between being a football coach and being a Christian," he wrote. "The number one thing a coach has to do is be himself; and if you're a Christian, then you'd better try not to be a hypocritical Christian. You'd better be consistent throughout whatever you do."

Dick Abel, a former FCA president, has seen that. "Tom is a leader of convictions, which gives him a consistency in his leadership," said Abel. "He knows who he is, and everyone else does as well. You are either a person of solid convictions or a chameleon, which means you don't know who you are or what you stand for."

Osborne knows both. "From the first time I met Tom, I realized he doesn't just say the first thing that crosses his mind," said Dal Shealy, also a former FCA president. "He thinks things through, formulates what he wants to say and then says it well. Tom is a man of his word and a man of high integrity. You can count on him to follow through on whatever commitment he makes.

"I noticed while we served on the FCA Board together that Tom always bathes things in prayer. He seeks wisdom from the Lord, whether it's about X's and O's or dealing with people. I saw him take meticulous notes at meetings because he wants to learn from anyone."

Shealy adds another familiar name in coaching to the Wooden-Smith list. "Tom was a strong leader but a servant leader as well. He was a lot like Tom Landry that way," Shealy said. "They were intensely focused on the task at hand, but they also knew how to enjoy life because they had joy in their lives."

Wayne Atcheson, the former sports information director at Alabama and first director of the Billy Graham Library in Charlotte, North Carolina, recalls the FCA conference in Estes Park in 1957. "No one knew then that this 19-year-old, tall, lean redhead would achieve greatness himself down the road," said Atcheson.

"It was my privilege to first know Tom when he was a graduate football assistant at Nebraska while I was serving on the national FCA staff in Kansas City. When he became a full-time assistant, he was the FCA chapter advisor, and we shared many FCA events together."

A chapter could be devoted to Atcheson's observations about Osborne.

"When you meet Tom, you meet a soft-spoken, sincere, kind, calm and humble man who is confident in who he is, so he concentrates on who you are," Atcheson said. "He comes off rock-solid by his very presence. He displays strong Midwestern values of strength, and deep down he has a very strong, competitive will to be the best. Not many football coaches have an earned doctorate in educational psychology either, and what an edge in guiding young men in the tender years.

"I never knew Tom as a boastful or proud person in the least. He was Nebraska-bred and raised and the perfect fit for the 'sea of red' in Memorial Stadium on Saturdays, a place of consecutive sellouts since 1962. He was another small-town boy that God set apart and used. He was as quick to talk to the farmers as he was a prize recruit. He suited the Nebraska corn-farmer fans to perfection. He was their kind of man. He probably even inspired farmers to over-achieve at harvest time.

"His no-nonsense demeanor led young men to work together as a team and relish in the fun and joy of being good. Tom was a great example of one that God chose, and he followed God's plan all the way. He was called to be a football coach and leader of collegiate men, but can't you see him just as well as a general in the U.S. Army, with his discipline and commitment in doing everything the right way?"

Atcheson's eloquent and insightful words as an outsider, so to speak, underscore the qualities that have made Osborne the leader he is because those qualities are apparent to anyone who takes the time to look.

"Perhaps the single greatest leadership trait for Tom came through his faith in Jesus Christ, from which came his strength, character, confidence and courage. Tom was always unashamed and unafraid when it came to sharing his faith with the masses. It's been a strong part of his entire life," said Atcheson. "Only God knows the influence he has imparted in the lives of athletes, coaches and the world of college football especially, and people of all walks of life. Psalm 40:4 fits Tom well. 'Blessed is the man who makes the Lord his trust,' and blessed are those who have been touched by Tom."

Mike Alden has been the director of athletics at Missouri since 1998. He is currently the third-longest tenured athletics director in the school's history and has overseen the Tigers' move to the Southeastern Conference. Like Osborne, his accomplishments have gone beyond the playing field, including facilities development and fund-raising. He currently serves as president of the Division IA Athletic Directors Association. "Tom Osborne is not a good leader; he's a great leader," Alden said. "He embodies integrity, humility and is a true servant leader. That's what separates him from so many others."

One member of the athletic department asked to remain anonymous in talking about Osborne, saying, "I am a person who is more comfortable in the background than in the spotlight." Osborne would say the same about himself. In any case, what that person said is worth including.

"It's hard for me to fully sum up what makes Tom a good leader. I believe that he is a good example of a servant leader. He is, more often than not, looking to serve someone else or the greater good in his decision-making, and I admire that. He also is someone that leads by example. He lives by the core values adopted by the Nebraska athletic department of integrity, trust, respect, teamwork, and loyalty. He genuinely cares for people that he works with and that work for him."

Back to Atcheson to finish this chapter, "Osborne continues to be a jewel for the state of Nebraska, demonstrating that leadership, his impeccable character and trust has a place badly needed in our nation today. Thank you Nebraska and Almighty God for Tom Osborne, a member of God's Hall of Fame."

Chapter Seven

COMMUNICATION: CALLING THE RIGHT PLAYS

"I truly believe that my mom and dad's legacy will be the state-wide mentoring program that they started years ago."

—SUZANNE HINCE,

Tom and Nancy Osborne's youngest daughter

A s was the case with most freshmen during Tom Osborne's 25 seasons as coach, Calvin Jones had to wait his turn. That's how the system worked, justified by the results.

For most of those 25 seasons, Nebraska fielded a freshman-junior varsity team, which Osborne used to allow players to make the transition from high school to college as well as gain a year's maturity. That was especially important for offensive linemen, who typically played on the freshman team then sat out a redshirt season before competing for playing time. That allowed for a physical maturity that came to characterize Husker offensive lines. Only two true freshmen offensive linemen played enough to earn letters under Osborne: Jake Young in 1986 and Will Shields in 1989.

Young, a center, was a two-time consensus All-American and an Academic All-American in 1989. Shields, a guard, was a unanimous All-American and Outland Trophy winner in 1992.

Nebraska discontinued its freshman-junior varsity program in February of 1991, forced to do so by an NCAA-mandated reduction in the number of assistant football coaches. The limit, instituted as a cost-cutting measure, went into effect in 1992. The Huskers' freshman-junior varsity team had its own coaches, something the new rules wouldn't allow, and played a five-game schedule in all but one of its 18 seasons under Osborne, compiling a record of 76-11-1.

In the beginning, Nebraska played freshman-junior varsity teams from other Big Eight schools, but a majority of those 88 games were against junior colleges and small college junior varsity teams willing to come to Lincoln, where most of the games were played. The Huskers' final freshman-junior varsity game was played at Memorial Stadium on Oct. 3, 1993, when, as a favor to Air Force coach Fisher DeBerry, Nebraska fielded a team to play the Air Force jayvees. The Huskers won. The teams had planned to play a second game in Colorado Springs in November. A snowstorm forced cancellation, however.

The freshman-junior varsity program was an example of Osborne's vision, a means of developing players, providing an opportunity not only for scholarship recruits but also for walk-ons who might otherwise have gotten lost in the shuffle.

But back to Jones, a freshman running back in the class of 1990, which included three offensive linemen who would clear the way for Osborne's first national championship in 1994, Zach Wiegert, Brenden Stai and Rob Zatechka, as well as defensive captains that season: Ed

Stewart and Terry Connealy; Zatechka and Wiegert were the offensive captains.

Jones, like Wiegert, Zatechka and Connealy, was from Nebraska, among the most publicized members of the class. He was a *USA Today* prep All-American at Omaha Central High School, which had produced several outstanding running backs, including Gale Sayers, who left Nebraska for Kansas, where he was an All-American before a Hall of Fame career with the Chicago Bears. Jones followed in Sayers' footsteps at Central, setting state Class A records for rushing yards in a game, season and career. He also was a state sprint champion, a prize recruit any way you looked at it.

Even so, Jones redshirted as a freshman, in part because another incoming freshman running back, Derek Brown, had sat out the previous season under NCAA-eligibility restrictions – Proposition 48. So Brown played in 1990 while Jones practiced on the scout team.

"I was the big recruit coming in on campus and I wanted to play," Jones recalled. "They (the coaches) told me they wanted to redshirt me. It was one of those decisions I didn't like, but it turned out to be the best thing for me because I had to go against the No. 1 defense. And, man, I'll tell you what, you learn how to get away from people real quick. There was no love down there on the scout team."

The week Nebraska played Colorado, Jones played the role of Buffaloes running back Eric Bieniemy in practice. And the week the Huskers played Oklahoma, he played the role of Sooners running back Mike Gaddis. "I wouldn't want anyone to go through what I went through," said Jones. "Wow, man. And then you had (defensive coordinator) Charlie McBride. 'Run the play, run where the cards say run, Jones.' 'OK, Coach, everybody knows where I'm running the ball.' Oh, man!"

The scout-team experience paid off. Jones earned second-team All-Big Eight recognition as a redshirted freshman, even though he was a back-up. In the Kansas game, he came off the bench after Brown was poked in the eye and rushed for a school-record 294 yards and six touchdowns. Jones was the Big Eight Offensive Player of the Year the next season as a sophomore. He and Brown both rushed for more than 1,000 yards and were known was the "We-backs," a play on the name of their position, I-back, and a reflection of the team-orientation emphasized by Osborne.

Though he missed two games with a knee injury as a junior, Jones still rushed for more than 1,000 yards for a second consecutive season and earned first-team all-conference honors. As Brown had done the year before, Jones bypassed his senior season and declared for the NFL draft. He was selected in the third round by the Los Angeles Raiders and spent three seasons in the league.

Jones, who finished his Nebraska career as the school's second-leading rusher all-time and still ranks fifth, was recruited by other schools, including UNLV, Tennessee and Colorado. But his affection for Nebraska could be traced to elementary school, when Huskers Turner Gill, Roger Craig and Dean Steinkuhler visited his fifth-grade class. "I remember they were in those red and white jerseys, and as kid growing up in north Omaha, Husker football and going to Memorial Stadium was so distant to me because I come from very humble beginnings," Jones said. "So to really see those guys in fifth grade, I wanted to be a Husker. That's kind of when I knew I was going to be a Husker."

He couldn't have known he'd have the opportunity, of course. That came later and had much to do with Osborne. Jones was raised by his grandmother, who "had always known Coach Osborne," said Jones. Not personally. Rather, "she watched from a distance," and knew what she saw was genuine.

What she saw was, well, let Jones explain. "I think the No. 1 thing was his faith. I think Coach Osborne was a man of faith," said Jones. "His faith makes him a great leader. He's trustworthy. He's very trustworthy. I've had to go to him on several occasions, some good, some bad, and he's always been there. I could trust him. What you see with Coach Osborne is what you get.

"How you saw him on TV, in the press conferences, I mean, that's truly what he was. But more importantly – I don't think he gets enough credit – for me and for others, he was the first father figure in our lives. So we would pretty much do what he said do. He recruited me, and then when you get to Nebraska, you deal with your position coach on a more regular basis than Coach Osborne. But I think from 'Jump Street,' man, he was a father figure for me because that figure hadn't been in my life."

Recruiting is the lifeblood of successful college football programs, and Nebraska recruits from coast to coast, a geographic necessity given the state's population base of fewer than 2 million. To put that in perspective, consider Osborne's second national championship team in 1995, regarded by many as being among the best in college football history. The Huskers' starting lineup for the 1996 Fiesta Bowl game against No. 2-ranked Florida included eight in-state players, with 10 other states represented. Osborne used 79 players in the 62-24 blowout, 45 of them from Nebraska. Sixteen other states were represented, from Texas to South Dakota and Montana, from New Jersey to California and Oregon.

A third of those, most of them from in-state, walked on from small Nebraska towns. But there's more about walk-ons earlier in this book. In marked contrast, Florida's starting lineup included only five out-of-state players. The recruiting advantages of being in a talent-rich state should be obvious.

"When I think about Coach Osborne, I think about a guy who could take kids from western Nebraska, and he could take kids from Louisiana, Florida, California, and bring them together, the black athletes not ever seeing white and the white athletes not ever seeing black," Jones said. "He could make them all fight for the same thing. That was one of the greatest things I thought Coach Osborne could do because I think it's rare for a coach to be able to do that."

As emphasized throughout this book, Osborne's leadership went far beyond the football field, however. He not only served as a father figure to his players but also encouraged them to be involved in the lives of youngsters in the community. To that end, he and wife Nancy created the TeamMates mentoring program, which now has more than 100 chapters, matching some 6,000 mentors with young people (grades 4 through 12) in communities in Iowa and California as well as in Nebraska.

"We even have a program going into South Dakota," Osborne said.

During his time as an assistant coach "I became more and more aware that many of our players were coming from less-stable homes," said Osborne. "These young men had grown up with no fathers or never knew their fathers, and this had created a lot of malfunction in their lives.

"One night, my wife Nancy was watching *60 Minutes* and saw a story about a man who had attended a suburban high school, which was now an inner-city school, facing a lot of problems. This man was willing to pay the way for these kids to go to college, and Nancy thought that was a terrific story. She asked me, 'What could we do?' And that launched our mentoring program.

"The concept was to use the influence of football to help youngsters in need."

The mission of the TeamMates program, as expressed on its website, is to "positively impact the world by inspiring youth to reach their full potential."

The program began in 1991, Jones' second year at Nebraska. Osborne asked for volunteers, and Jones was among those who stepped up. Twenty-five boys from middle schools in Lincoln were matched with players. The numbers show the program's success: 22 stayed in the program, 20 graduated from high school, and 18 continued on to post-secondary education.

"We were encouraged and decided to expand the program," Osborne said.

It grew quickly. In 1997, it expanded through Lincoln's St. Mark's United Methodist Church and the Lincoln Public Schools system and included 160 volunteer mentors, no longer just football players. A year later, the program was formalized statewide, affiliating with the Nebraska Community Foundation, with 12 chapters and 440 youngsters matched with mentors.

"We discovered that with 85 percent of the matches, school attendance improved and with 75 percent of the matches, behavior improved, with less gang involvement and fewer teenage pregnancies. In addition, academic results were much better across the board," said Osborne.

In any case, as mentioned earlier, Jones was among the players who volunteered to mentor in 1991. "I wanted to give back and try to help another kid that was like me," he said. "I wanted to give back and try to help somebody that just needed a little hope and encouragement."

That's also the reason the organization he founded, Omaha-based Forever A Husker, sponsors events for youngsters. "After what I've been through in my life, the best thing for me is to give back," said Jones. "I've been blessed beyond my imagination, and for me to be able to come through what I've come through, there's no stronger message that I have than bringing hope to some of these youths that don't see hope in the community."

The social problems in the north Omaha neighborhood where he grew up have worsened over the years. But "it's not only north Omaha," Jones said. "It's central and western Nebraska. Everybody's looking for hope and motivation, so that's what I try to do."

Osborne was the model for his mission.

Shields, mentioned earlier in this chapter, was another of those Huskers who volunteered to mentor in 1991. He was a junior at the time and well on his way to earning a place in the hearts of Nebraska fans, who appreciated not only his play but also his steady, businesslike approach.

Like his head coach, Shields was not someone who seemed to enjoy the spotlight for what he did, even though what he did inevitably drew the spotlight his way, despite his being an offensive lineman. The best of Nebraska's offensive linemen have never labored in anonymity. Check the all-time list of Outland Trophy winners. Nebraska has produced nine, with six of them awarded to offensive lineman, including Dave Rimington's two (1981-82).

All five of the Huskers' Outland Trophy-winning offensive linemen played for Osborne, and four of the five were three-time, first-team all-conference honorees – including Shields, who started the final 36 games of his career and was a unanimous All-American as a senior in 1992.

Shields was recruited out of Lawton, Oklahoma, and picked Nebraska not only because of its football tradition but also because of its emphasis on academics – which was Osborne's emphasis.

He was a third-round NFL draft pick of the Kansas City Chiefs in 1993, the 74th player selected, and continued his success with the

Chiefs, starting a franchise-record 223 consecutive games over 14 seasons and was selected to 12 consecutive Pro Bowls.

Osborne "had a great staff and let them coach the team," said Shields, who is enshrined in the College Football Hall of Fame. "He was the guider of the ship and had his influence on the whole program. But it was not always his dictating what needed to be done.

"As players, we liked that approach. His assistants did the coaching, which allowed Coach Osborne to spend time with his players, discussing school and life issues."

School and life issues were important to Shields, who has built two successful businesses in the Kansas City area: 68 Inside Sports Health and Wellness and 68 Inside Sports Indoor Training Facility. He's also a contributor to I've Got Heart, a program in which students write letters to inspire hospital patients. But his most significant contribution to his community is the Will to Succeed Foundation.

He and wife Senia, whom he met in Nebraska when she was an exchange student from Denmark, established the foundation in 1993, his first year with the Chiefs. The foundation "seeks to guide and inspire, empower and improve the lives of those less fortunate by providing financial, educational and other everyday resources to those identified as most in need," its website says.

The foundation's focus is abused, battered and neglected women and children. Since it was established, it has helped more than 100,000 individuals.

In 2003, Shields was named the NFL's Walter Payton Man of the Year.

Steve Warren was recruited out of Springfield, Missouri, and played his first two seasons at Nebraska under Osborne. Like Shields, he earned a letter as a true freshman, in 1996. He was a defensive tackle and a regular on the 1997 national championship team, starting two games because of injury.

Warren earned first-team All-Big 12 recognition in 1999 on a Frank Solich-coached team that finished 12-1 and ranked No. 3 nationally. Only a 24-20 loss at Texas, avenged in the Big 12 championship game, probably kept the Huskers from playing for a national championship.

He left Nebraska one semester before graduating in order to prepare for the NFL draft. Ironically, like Shields, he was a third-round selection, the 74th player picked, by the Green Bay Packers. His NFL career was cut short by injury, however, and he returned to Nebraska to complete a degree in sociology.

Also like Shields, Warren then got involved in the community, a decision, he has said, influenced by Osborne as well as by his parents.

In 2006, he established the D.R.E.A.M. program – Developing Relationships through Education, Athletics and Mentoring – in Omaha to "expand opportunities for at-risk youth by providing positive role models who emphasize values, good character and the importance of education," its website says.

It began as an after-school program at one Omaha elementary school. It now has chapters in Springfield, Missouri, and California.

Osborne "was a consistent leader," said Warren. "He was the same every day, always even-keel. You couldn't tell if he was rattled or upset or over-excited. That left a big impression on me. I watched closely and learned from him. He handled his job the right way, and that played an inspirational role in my life. I learned that leadership is an every-day job.

"Above all, I learned that Coach treated all of his players the same way. He'd stop and hold conversations with all of us, regardless of our rank on the team."

Warren also has established a separate sports-performance academy for training youngsters, with an emphasis on leadership and character.

Matt Davison arrived at Nebraska the year after Warren. "Coach had a way of getting us to buy into the team concept," Davison said. "He got a bunch of Nebraska kids together and got us to believe collectively we could accomplish great things."

Not all were Nebraska kids, of course. But a dozen starters in 1997, Davison's freshman season, were from in-state, as were many who contributed to Osborne's third national championship.

Davison was from Tecumseh, Nebraska, a small community less than an hour's drive east of Lincoln. He was a scholarship recruit and played immediately, without redshirting. He was a split end, and though he wasn't a starter, he made arguably the season's most memorable play.

The Huskers traveled to Columbia, Missouri, to play their ninth game. They were undefeated and ranked No. 1. Most Nebraska fans of a certain age can recount the particulars of what follows as surely as they will pronounce Osborne's name properly, "Oz-burn" rather than "Oz-born."

The Huskers trailed 38-31 with 1:02 remaining, no timeouts and the ball at their 33-yard line. As were all but Osborne's early teams, Nebraska was heavily run-oriented in 1997. It led the nation in rushing and averaged more than three times as many rushing yards as passing yards.

The Huskers' leading receiver had just 14 catches. Davison was tied for third, with 11, and led the team in receiving yards with 232.

Even so, quarterback Scott Frost passed Nebraska down the field, 10 passes, five of them complete. The fourth completion took the ball to the Missouri 12-yard line, first-and-10. Two incompletions left the Huskers with a third down and only 7 seconds remaining.

Frost's 10th pass was intended for wingback Shevin Wiggins at the goal line. The ball deflected off Wiggins – or was kicked – and Davison made a diving catch in the middle of the end zone. The clock showed 00:00. Kris Brown's extra-point kick tied the score at 38, forcing overtime.

Nebraska won in overtime, 45-38, to keep its unbeaten season alive, and after a decisive Orange Bowl victory against Tennessee, the Huskers were voted No. 1 in the coaches' poll.

An interesting footnote or piece of trivia if you will, Davison didn't get credit for the dramatic catch on the official play-by-play, compiled by the Missouri sports information office. Osborne's teams had enough players that many wore duplicate jersey numbers. Davison and senior free safety Eric Warfield both wore No. 3. So the play-by-play said of the tying touchdown: "E. Warfield crossing pass from S. Frost for 12 yards to the MISSOURI0, 1ST DOWN NU, TOUCHDOWN, clock 00:00."

The catch gave Davison instant celebrity, but it wasn't the only thing that defined his Husker career. He earned four letters and Big 12 honorable mention three times, again even though Nebraska threw the ball sparingly under Frank Solich, Osborne's successor, as well. Davison was a three-time Academic All-Big 12 honoree and two-time Academic All-District VII selection. And despite the demands of football and schoolwork, he still found time to play a semester of basketball, 15 games.

"The passion of the Nebraska players in the locker room and practice field was something Coach used to his advantage," said Davison, now a color analyst on the Husker radio network. "It rubbed off on the out-of-state guys, and they began to realize, 'Wow! This means a lot to these guys.' Those Nebraska natives brought it every day in practice, and it was amazing to watch. Tom Osborne's message to us was short and sweet: 'If you all do your jobs, we can accomplish great things at a very high level.'"

Davison has carried that attitude beyond the field of play, establishing the Creating Captains Foundation, which "teaches young people to lead in our nation's schools and communities," its website says. The four core values are character, courage, leadership and respect.

Those qualities are the subject of this book. And here are testimonies from more Huskers.

Tony Davis preceded Davison from Tecumseh. Among his nicknames was the "Tecumseh Tornado," but the most common was "Tough Tony," an appropriately descriptive name. Davis began his career as an I-back, switching to fullback as a junior. His first varsity season was Osborne's first as head coach, a point of pride. "I was the first tailback for Coach on his first team," said Davis, who became just the third Husker to rush for 1,000 yards that season. "I remember years later going to his retirement party. What a humble guy. He said, 'I owe my first three or four teams an apology. You actually carried me.'"

Davis was the MVP in Osborne's first two bowl games, victories against Texas in the Cotton Bowl and Florida in the Sugar Bowl. He also finished his career as the leading rusher in Husker history. He was a fourth-round NFL draft pick and played six seasons with Cincinnati and Tampa Bay.

"Tom's greatest asset as a coach was the consistency that controlled his life. His outlook was, 'Here's what I believe. Here's how I'll live. Here's how I'll coach these guys,'" Davis said. "We would run 250 practice plays. In fact, we'd run the same play 10 to 15 times a day until we'd perfected it.

"That's how we wore teams down, and it was all based on Tom's teaching of consistency. What he was really teaching us was that if you do the same fundamental things in life, over and over again, you'll have a good life."

For Osborne, it was never just about football.

Gerry Gdowski knows something about consistency and acting on principle. He didn't redshirt, by choice. If he had, he almost certainly would have started for two seasons instead of one, 1989, because until then he was playing behind Steve Taylor, who became a starter in his sophomore season.

Gdowski came from Fremont, Nebraska, where he was the state's boys high school athlete of the year, excelling in track and field as well as football. His mom was a school teacher and his dad a coach, so he had his priorities in order from the start. He was an Academic All-American as a senior, in addition to the Big Eight Conference Co-Offensive Player of the Year.

Going into his senior season at Nebraska, Gdowski's statistics included 6-of-10 passes completed for 72 yards and 286 rushing yards and four touchdowns on 35 carries. As a senior, he was as productive as just about any quarterback ever coached by Osborne, passing for 19 touchdowns with only two interceptions and rushing for 925 yards and 13 touchdowns. The 925 rushing yards were the most-ever by a Husker quarterback at the time. He averaged 7.3 yards per carry.

"The thing I thought made Tom a good leader was his consistency in his approach and message," said Gdowski, now the assistant head coach, co-offensive coordinator and quarterbacks coach for Solich at Ohio. "I was able to see him as a player and as a grad assistant coach. "I always knew by what day of the week it was what we were going to cover in meetings and practice that day.

"It seemed it was about the process of how we were going to approach that week's game. It did not matter if we were playing Oklahoma or a non-conference game, that process from Monday to

Saturday was the same. He did not change his approach or personality because of who we were playing that week. That allowed coaches and players to stay focused on the task at hand and not get too caught up on any outside pressures or distractions. I think that is why you rarely saw one of his teams get beat by a lesser opponent."

Rarely? Try once in 25 years. Under Osborne, as noted earlier in this book, the Huskers lost to only one team that finished the season with a losing record. Iowa State upset them 19-10 at Ames, Iowa, in 1992.

Nebraska didn't lose to any opponent during quarterback Jerry Tagge's final two seasons, and to only two during his first season. The Huskers' record was 33-2-1, with national championships in 1970 and 1971, when Tagge started every game, after sharing time with Van Brownson for the first two seasons.

Tagge earned All-America honors in 1971, when he was a co-captain, along with defensive back Jim Anderson, a high school teammate in Green Bay, Wisconsin. Tagge got to know Osborne through the daily quarterback meetings Osborne set up a couple of seasons before.

"Tom was so consistent with his discipline it was about mechanical," said Tagge. "I had lunch with him every day at noon. He went over everything with us, always stressing fundamentals and doing everything the right way. When I got in the game, it seemed so easy because Tom had explained things so well. He had a good way of communicating.

"There might be 2 minutes left in the game and Nebraska was up by 40 points or more. The third team was in there and Coach would still have his headset on, still calling the plays. He always had a purpose – to get the maximum out of his players."

Osborne "never yelled at us or embarrassed us in front of our teammates," Tagge said. "If he needed to address an issue, he'd do it behind closed doors. We respected him so much for that. Tom never cut a corner in life or in football. The small things in both areas were important to him. We looked up to him and wanted to play for him, and our mothers wanted us to spend four or five years under his tutelage."

Steve Runty was another who sat in quarterback meetings with Osborne, and Tagge for one season. Runty was a sophomore on the 1971 national championship team. He walked on from Ogallala, Nebraska, and earned two letters as a back-up. However, he has the distinction of starting Osborne's first game as head coach because Dave Humm was injured and directing the 40-13 victory.

"He was a little nervous about that, but I wasn't because I'd been around forever," said Runty, who also scored the first touchdown of the Osborne era. "As I look back, Tom was more prepared than UCLA that day to play the game. He called a better game, and all the plays he called worked. Everyone believed in him because he was always so well-prepared."

The man who would start the TeamMates mentoring program nearly 20 years later "has been a mentor to thousands of us over six decades, almost" Runty said. "He never tried to force his faith on any of us, but to this day, I try to be more Christ-like because of Tom. Now I realize that he had Jesus Christ in his heart, which gave him a powerful love for people.

"He loved all of his players, from All-Americans to a whole bunch of walk-ons. He made all of us feel like stars. Whenever I got an opportunity to play, I was ready to roll because I felt like a genuine part of the team. Tom lived his faith and didn't just talk about it. I think about the man a lot."

Dan Schmidt redshirted in 1973, after starting for the freshman team 1972, Devaney's last season as coach. He came from North Platte, Nebraska, and started his final two seasons at offensive guard.

"I was there for Tom's first team meeting as head coach," Schmidt said. "I saw him grow as a leader in his first five years. Consistency was his Hallmark as a top-level leader. He was always the same as a person and preached the same stuff to his players. That settles in with you after a while and sticks with us to this day. I can still hear his voice: 'You've got to do your job. Take care of the ball. Don't get cocky. This team can beat you.'"

Ed Stewart was a co-captain on Osborne's first national championship team in 1994, a consensus All-American linebacker and finalist for the Dick Butkus Award. He was recruited out of Chicago as a defensive back and was reluctant to switch positions to linebacker.

Stewart's move was part of a change in defensive philosophy that contributed significantly to Osborne's three national championships. The Huskers went to an attacking 4-3 defense, which allowed them to better deal with the warm-weather passing attacks they faced in bowl games.

"Tom let his coaches coach because he believed in them and his players," said Stewart, an assistant commissioner for the Big 12 Conference. "He never embarrassed anyone; if he had something to say, he'd say it in private, behind closed doors. Tom was interested in you as a person. As a result, we worked harder because of those things. The true test of leadership is getting people to do more and do it better. That's how Tom inspired and empowered people."

Several former players have talked about how Osborne brought together players from different backgrounds, big cities and small towns. Terry Connealy, also a co-captain on the 1994 national championship team, was from Hyannis, Nebraska, where he played eight-man football in high school. His dad was a western-Nebraska rancher and had been a Husker in the 1950s.

Connealy earned four letters as a defensive tackle, earning first-team All-Big Eight recognition as a junior. He was a three-time academic all-conference selection and a two-time, first-team Academic All-American – one of two on the 1994 team. Offensive tackle Rob Zatechka also was a two-time, first-team Academic All-American, as well as a co-captain.

Osborne "was very consistent and even-keeled," said Connealy, an analyst for the Husker radio network for a time. "His highs were never too high and his lows never too low. He was crystal clear on his expectations for his players. He always had a plan and told us, 'If you follow it, you'll be successful.' Coach led by example and as a result was a tremendous leader."

Eric Stokes, from Lincoln (Nebraska) East High School, was a sophomore defensive back on Osborne's 1994 national championship team, during a college career hampered by injuries. He began his junior season at cornerback, starting the first two games, and finished as a free safety, starting there as a senior. He also earned academic all-conference recognition twice.

He was a fifth-round draft pick of the Seattle Seahawks in 1997. Again, injuries interceded and he played in the NFL only briefly. But he remained in the league as a scout for the Seahawks, opting to do that rather than return to Nebraska to be a graduate assistant. The decision was difficult but as it turned out, the right one. After a dozen years with the Seahawks, Stokes was named director of college scouting for the Tampa Bay Buccaneers in May of 2012.

Osborne "was always consistent in all areas of his life," Stokes said. "His message, demeanor and personality never wavered or changed. His highest highs were never too high, and his lowest lows were never too low. Coach Osborne's poise and self-control never changed, and I never heard him raise his voice. It's hard to find that in football coaches, which made Coach incredibly unique. We could always look to him and know that everything was going to be OK."

Chad Kelsay played on the 1995 and 1997 national championship teams as a rush end, the 1995 team as a true freshman. He was a first-team Academic All-American as a senior in 1998, after earning second-team honors in 1997, and a co-captain.

Osborne's leadership "was not flamboyant, with a lot of Knute Rockne, rah-rah stuff," said Kelsay, director of business development for the Omaha Truck Center. "Coach Osborne's approach was more stoic and businesslike. He didn't yell, scream or cuss, and that atmosphere would radiate down through the whole team. Coach always had a prepared approach to the game, and 85 to 90 percent of that preparation was in place before the team ever went on the field. His pre-game talks would be boring to the average fan. They were always focused on preparation in all phases of the game.

"He'd go over every piece of the game and any possibility that might come up that day. Coach was a professor at heart and was always teaching."

Osborne "could relate to his players at all levels and get the most out of them. However, he wanted full development in other parts of our lives – academic success, character development, a good spiritual foundation and involvement in the community," Kelsay said. "By and large, most of his players have become well-rounded and successful contributors to society."

Stan Parker is a co-founder, along with current Husker running backs coach Ron Brown, of the statewide Christian Ministry Mission Nebraska. He was recruited out of East High School in Bellevue, Nebraska, as a tight end but moved to offensive tackle and then to offensive guard, where he was a part-time starter as a junior and full-time starter as a senior, in 1986, when he was a co-captain.

"Coach had a genuine concern for his players," said Parker. "As a (redshirted) freshman, I was doing my pre-practice stretching when Coach came over to me. He knew my name, asked about my injury situation and wanted to know what was going on in my life. That never changed for the next four years."

Parker missed his freshman season because of a knee injury suffered in the Nebraska Shrine Bowl high school all-star game.

Osborne "cared about us as individuals and treated us with respect. Through good times or frustrating ones, I never saw Coach attack, demean or belittle a player," Parker said. "I never saw him put down one of us by word, tone or look. That's so rare in coaches of any sport.

"Coach led us by his influence. His physical carriage was part of that, but he didn't just talk his philosophy of life; he lived it. You just wanted to follow him and please him because of who he was. You didn't need big speeches from Coach to do your best for him. It tore you up if you disappointed him. That's all I needed to stay motivated."

Tom Welter was a member of the same recruiting class as Parker. He came from Yankton, South Dakota, a 6-foot-6, 250-pound lineman with a 225-pound bench press and 5.65-second speed in the 40-yard dash. He played offensive tackle, and by his senior season, he weighed 280 pounds and had increased his bench press to 365 pounds while dropping his 40-yard dash time to 5.26 seconds. Such development in the Husker strength and conditioning program was typical.

Welter didn't play enough to letter as a third-year sophomore, but he started his final two seasons and was first-team All-Big Eight as well as an Academic All-American in 1986.

Osborne "was always calm under pressure and in every setting – when the score was tied late in the game, in the players' dining room, or discussing academics one-on-one," said Welter. "He was a calming figure for his players, the Nebraska fans and the entire state. Coach always stayed the course because he knew his recipe worked."

Jim Skow was among the best pass rushers in Husker history, a defensive tackle in the mid-1980s from Roncalli High School in Omaha. Like Welter, he made marked improvement in the strength and conditioning program. His weight increased from 215 to 250 pounds while his time in the 40-yard dash dropped from 5.06 seconds as a freshman to 4.91 seconds as a senior.

The 6-foot-3 Skow relied on that speed and his strength – he was among the strongest players on the team, with a 415-pound bench press – because he wasn't overly heavy for a lineman. He started only three games in his first two seasons. Even so, Husker defensive coordinator Charlie McBride called him possibly "the most under-rated defensive player in the league" prior to his senior season.

Skow was credited with 15 sacks that season, justifying McBride's words.

Osborne "had the will to win, and you could tell by the look in his eyes; he exuded that. He was totally focused on winning, and he passes that on to his players," said Skow, who went on to play seven seasons in the NFL, with 24 career sacks – including 21.5 in the last four seasons.

Danny Noonan, a middle guard, was overshadowed by Skow as a junior in 1985, even though he was a second-team All-Big Eight selection. He emerged with Skow gone to the NFL in 1986, earning unanimous All-America honors and being named Big Eight Athlete of the Year.

Noonan was a first-round draft pick of the Dallas Cowboys and played seven seasons in the NFL.

"Tom Osborne was not a rah-rah type leader," Noonan said, echoing many others. "He had a quiet confidence about him, and when he talked, people listened. You could hear a pin drop, and Tom didn't have to say a lot to get that response. We all respected what he said because we knew he'd follow through on it. As a result, Tom had all of us on the same page and pulling together as one."

Tom Banderas played tight end and caught only 16 passes during his career (1985-87). But 10 of those catches went for touchdowns, an indication of how Osborne's run-oriented offense was able to capitalize on play-action passes.

"If I could do it all over again, I'd come back to Nebraska to play for Coach Osborne," said Banderas, who was recruited from Oak Grove, Missouri. "That speaks to the character of the man.

"Coach had a consistency to his behavior. He didn't have to yell, curse and kick things around. His philosophy was that you were playing for Nebraska and 'if I have to yell and scream on game day, that means we didn't prepare you properly during the week.' We were not a helter-skelter team out there. We played with a consistency because that's how Coach trained us to play. Everybody wants to win, but if we were well-prepared and lost, that was OK."

Banderas is in the insurance business in Lincoln, and his son Josh was recruited by Nebraska.

"When Coach retired, it seems Nebraska lost its calm demeanor and consistency," he said. "For years we worked hard and knew what we were doing, and we felt we had a better overall program than our opponents. You can hope to win – you've got to win, period.

"Tom's calm, consistent leadership was the key. It didn't matter whether we were up by three touchdowns or down by three touchdowns, Coach was the same. He never panicked. He always remained cool, calm and collected no matter how much he might have been churning on the inside."

Kris Van Norman says much the same thing as Banderas. Osborne "made you believe you were going to win every game," Van Norman said. "We'd walk out on that field believing it would take a tremendous upset to beat us. Coach was an unbelievable competitor, who wanted to win badly."

Van Norman came from Minden, another small town in Nebraska, and earned three letters as a safety, starting as a senior in 1982 and earning second-team Academic All-America honors. He was a two-time Academic All-Big Eight selection.

Osborne's philosophy "was to take care of the things you can control," said Van Norman. "We were always thoroughly prepared, with every detail covered completely. Coach believed that you don't stay the same. You're either getting better or you're getting worse.

"He challenged us to try to improve a little each day and over time that will add up."

Henry Waechter transferred to Nebraska from Waldorf (Iowa) Junior College, where he was a junior college All-American, and started at defensive tackle for two seasons (1980-81).

"Coach taught all of us about the importance of being honest and truthful," said Waechter, who was a seventh-round draft pick of the Chicago Bears and played six seasons in the NFL. "He handled himself in such a manner that I hope I can be similar to how Tom does it."

Osborne was a role model for most of those who played for him. Mike Minter was a member of his 1992 recruiting class, coming from Lawton, Oklahoma. He was only the third Husker football scholarship recruit from Oklahoma at the time. The first was Victor Stachmus from McAlester in 1988, the second Shields, mentioned earlier in this chapter, also from Lawton in 1989.

Minter earned the starting job at free safety as a third-year sophomore in 1994 and was regarded as the quarterback of the defense. But he suffered an ACL injury in the second game of the season at Texas Tech, and his loss was considered a serious blow to Nebraska's national title hopes, coming off a 1993 season in which the Huskers had come within a missed field goal at the end of the Orange Bowl game against Florida State of winning Osborne's first national championship.

Minter returned to start on the 1995 national championship team at rover and was a co-captain as a senior in 1996, when he earned first-team All-Big 12 recognition.

"Coach treated all of his players the same, and it didn't matter if you were an All-American or a walk-on. Every player got the same respect," said Minter. "We all thought Coach treated us fairly. Coach always knew what to say and when to say it to you. He knew his craft, too. If a coach knows what he's doing, his players will follow closely."

Minter was a second-round draft pick of the Carolina Panthers in 1997 and played 10 NFL seasons, all with the Panthers, and in one Super Bowl, against the New England Patriots following the 2003 season. He coached three seasons at First Assembly Christian Academy in Concord, North Carolina, his record was 35-4 with two state championships. He was an assistant coach for one season at Johnson C. Smith University. After serving as special-teams coach for former Husker Turner Gill at Liberty University, Minter was named head coach at Campbell University in late November of 2012.

"At the start of my freshman year, Coach Osborne said to the entire squad, 'It's good if you can make it, but remember to always give back.' That statement has been stuck in my mind for a long time," said Minter, who is a successful businessman as well as a football coach.

He is CEO of Minter Enterprises, "a multi-faceted business impacting real estate development, general contracting and construction, business consultation, publishing, public speaking engagements and a non-profit organization focused on youth development," the website says.

The non-profit organization, Minter Community, includes a mentoring program with a stated goal of identifying youngsters ages 7 through 18 "who are going to have a turbulent transition to adulthood and offer a positive support system to avoid the pitfalls that can derail their lives."

"It's important to give back to others and not just dwell on yourself," Minter said. "Give back your time, your knowledge and experiences, and your money.

"That's how Tom Osborne preached, and that's how we played."

EPILOGUE

Randy York was named Nebraska Sportswriter of the Year six times during 19 years at the Lincoln (Nebraska) Journal and Star, *serving as prep sports editor and then covering Tom Osborne and the Husker beat as a writer, columnist and assistant sports editor. He worked for 22½ years as a manager and director in Corporate Communications and was the managing editor of Sprint's corporate magazine and the company's annual report before returning to Nebraska. He is now Senior Writer and Director of Creative Services for Huskers.com/Web Services and works directly with Osborne.*

First and foremost, I think Coach Osborne is a great leader because of the kind of person he is. He's a man of faith and principles, and he's very open about both because they are the guideposts for the way he lives, acts and operates every day. He's very humble about his faith and very soft spoken about the principles that drive him. He never forces his views on anyone or acts as if he has all the answers. He's the type of man who's at ease talking to those who have great power or those who have none. He works and leads by example and fully accepts and embraces being a role model for others.

Faith and principles drive every leadership bone in his body. He's bright, articulate, disciplined and consistent. Even at 75, he's like an Eagle Scout. He's always prepared—for anything. I compare Coach Osborne to John Wooden, a man he considered to be both a friend and a mentor. Both coaches were remarkable winners, but neither was driven by winning itself. Like Wooden, Coach Osborne is an incredibly strong listener, a lost art indeed in a Facebook, Twitter-kind of world. When Coach talks, people listen, and when they talk, he listens, not just to hear, but to understand how they think, so he can base his decisions on disciplined logic and common sense analysis.

Coach Osborne loved his players, and they loved him – from the Heisman and Outland Trophy winners to the walk-ons who rarely played but gave everything they had to be part of something extraordinary. Coach knew those walk-ons personally and respected the sacrifices they were willing to make. He knew their parents and often would ask how they're doing. Coach was instrumental in every player respecting the role he was given, so he could set the tone for others. No one wanted to let their coach down. Players from the 1960s, '70s, '80s and '90s will tell you how Osborne prepared them for life every bit as much as he prepared them for football.

Somehow, even back in the '60s, an IQ that helped Coach achieve his doctorate in Educational Psychology convinced him that football could be inextricably linked to faith and family because success in any of those three areas required some of the same personal values. Game Day was Coach's weekly report card, but Life Commitment was his passionate, relentless quest for what became a Hall-of-Fame career that enabled him to share his faith, love his family and excel like few others. No one in college football history has averaged more than 10 wins and fewer than 2 losses over 25 consecutive seasons.

Four words spring to mind looking at Coach's quarter-century record of 255 wins, 49 losses, 3 ties and 3 national championships: "unheard of" and "never again." It's going to be a long time before another coach wins 60 of 63 games and 3 national championships and has 1 national runner-up finish in the same 5-year span. Coach was never driven by fame, fortune, power or greed. A major chunk of what he earned as a head coach was shared consistently with the staff that supported him. That's part of the reason why his assistant coaches were just as loyal to him as his players were. They would all run through a wall for Coach Osborne.

Coach has written books that carry titles reflective of his view on life: *Beyond the Final Score: There's More to Life than the Game*; *More Than Winning: Secrets to Becoming a Leader*; *Faith in the Game: Lessons on Football, Work and Life*; *On Solid Ground*. I carry in my briefcase a pocket-sized version of Coach's *Secrets to Becoming a Leader* book, and it includes a quote from Wooden on the front cover: "Tom Osborne has always gone beyond the final score, achieving competitive greatness with integrity, hard work, selfless sacrifice and strong faith." My take: Osborne knows what matters most, and it's a big part of his legacy.

After serving three terms as a U.S. Congressman representing Nebraska, Coach Osborne returned to his alma mater as athletic director in 2007. Within months, he brought together every employee in the athletic department, so each had a voice in forming a mission to serve student-athletes, coaches, staff and fans. Every employee could vote on every word and every value. In the end, every decision, action and purpose would be driven by five core values – integrity, trust, respect, teamwork and loyalty. Coach Osborne bases his own leader-ship style on many of those same principles, so the sense of unity was consistent across the board.

When you work *with* Coach Osborne and *for* him, you see on a daily basis how he applies those five values and why they equal success. While some might see Coach as fairly set in his ways, I see that as an endorsement, not an indictment because he's always listening, analyzing, doing his homework and coming up with solutions that are both innovative and stand the test of time. That's why Coach has been productive and stayed as relevant in 2012 as he was in 1962, the same year he joined Bob Devaney's coaching staff and helped Nebraska start its ongoing NCAA record of selling out home football games for 50 consecutive years.

Looking back at Coach's decade-by-decade contributions, I marvel at how he met all the challenges and still managed to have such incredible balance in his own life. He has one speed – full-steam ahead – yet always appears calm and at peace. He meditates every morning and spends meaningful time with his wife, kids and their families – from weekends at the family farm with wild turkeys and favorite fishing spots to lifetime memories on a South African safari. Such experiences explain why he's never in a hurry, yet always focused on something that will benefit the athletic department, the university, the state or society as a whole.

Coach Osborne doesn't just write books about lessons in leadership and life. He lives by the same wisdom he writes about. He's the kind of leader who stays inside the box when it's the right thing to do, but he's more than willing to go outside the box when he thinks it's required. The way he's resurrected Nebraska's athletic facilities is testimony to his leadership. With systematic innovation, he's led the charge to build a new Student-Athlete Center and, at the same time, give Nebraska football and basketball extreme makeovers. His leadership also has benefited almost every other sport with meaningful improvements that enhance recruiting.

Coach Osborne is one of those rare leaders who can always honor others without ever betraying himself. I think he honed that skill decades ago when he agreed to serve on the boards of directors of companies he respected. At board meetings, other directors couldn't believe how a head football coach could know their business almost as well as they knew it themselves. His penchant for data and statistics served him well as a board member. While immersing himself in someone else's business, he became a subject matter expert, making it fairly easy for him to gain the trust and earn the respect of other leaders he helped lead.

The TeamMates mentoring program that Tom and wife Nancy started 21 years ago began with a recommendation, was based on a simple question he asked his football team and became a reality when 22 players volunteered. The program now has more than 100 chapters in communities serving nearly 6,000 students from grade school to high school – in both urban and rural areas. It's an outgrowth of a vision Osborne inherently understands because his grandfather had a mentor that shaped his family's life. Coach knows the ripple effect a mentor can create and believes strongly in doing something for someone who can't do anything in return.

Coach invests himself to serve others with that same philosophical foundation. He believes in affirming and encouraging those who are already strong and blessed and doing the same for those who are disadvantaged and struggling. It's the essence of who he is as a man, husband, father, grandfather, coach, Congressman, athletic director and leader. However stressful a situation can get, Coach never loses his composure or his compassion. He stays calm, cool, collected and true to his character. It all comes from his faith and the beliefs that guide every personal and professional decision he makes.

I've never seen anyone so humble walk into a room and command it, even when the sound is silence. Coach doesn't have to say anything to get anyone's attention. He radiates respect, and he's earned it because of the way he sees the world, operates in it and manages to stay above the fray. In politics, he would not compromise his principles, and he would not change his position on something just to gain extra percentage points in a media poll. I worked in Corporate America for more than 22 years and in my opinion, there are very few leaders with Coach's commanding combination of competitive drive and character-based leadership.

Coach has a proven track record in every challenge he takes on because he's all about process, preparation and principles, and here's the best part about his leadership: He thinks all of us can improve and succeed if we combine those qualities with good, old-fashioned hard work. A lot of coaches used and still use John Wooden's *Pyramid of Success* as the cornerstones of their philosophy. I don't know of anyone besides Wooden himself who has brought those qualities to life like Coach Osborne. I think Coach Wooden was the best coach in the history of sports, and I think Coach Osborne was one of the best leaders right behind him.

Like Steven Covey, the author of the *Seven Habits of Highly Effective People*, Coach Osborne always has believed in beginning with the end in mind, and it seems no small coincidence that he envisioned something beyond the 2013 last major expansion to Memorial Stadium. Included in that new East Stadium will be significantly large areas to accommodate two major research initiatives – one that the University of Nebraska will oversee and the other that NU's Athletic Department will direct. One of the first athletic research projects in Big Ten Conference history will be a game-changing monitoring system for strength and conditioning training.

Nebraska is recognized as the Father of American Athletic Strength and Conditioning Training. The reason the Huskers own that honor is because a young assistant coach proposed to his head coach that Nebraska be the first collegiate or professional football team to hire a strength coach. Osborne walked into Devaney's office with Boyd Epley, who convinced Devaney that hiring him made sense – mainly because Osborne's research was behind it. A half century later, a visionary Osborne is as relevant today as he was in the 1960s, begging this question: Could there be a more meaningful milestone for one of the greatest leaders of our time?

ACKNOWLEDGMENTS

With deep appreciation we acknowledge the support and guidance of the following people who helped make this book possible:

Special thanks to Alex Martins, Dan DeVos and Rich DeVos of the Orlando Magic.

Thanks also to my writing partner Mike Babcock for his superb contributions in shaping this manuscript.

Hats off to three dependable associates—my trusted and valuable colleague Andrew Herdliska, my creative consultant Ken Hussar, and my ace typist Fran Thomas.

Hearty thanks also go to my friends at the Advantage Media family. Thank you all for believing that we had something important to share and for providing the support and the forum to say it. Special thanks to founder Adam Witty for your continued support and encouragement.

And finally, special thanks and appreciation go to my wife, Ruth, and my supportive children and grandchildren. They are truly the backbone of my life.

—PAT WILLIAMS

THE AUTHORS ACKNOWLEDGE AND
THANK ALL THOSE WHO CONTRIBUTED TO
Tom Osborne on Leadership:

Dick Abel

George Achola

Mike Alden

Barry Alvarez

George Andrews

Mike Arthur

Tom Ash

Wayne Atcheson

Tom Banderas

Bill Bennett

Bill Bobbora

Bobby Bowden

Ralph Brown

Ron Brown

Don Bryant

Michael Castle

Tim Clare

Terry Connealy

Barney Cotton

Roger Craig

George Darlington

Tony Davis

Matt Davison

Jim Delany

Bill Doleman

Bruce Dunning

Lavell Edwards

Boyd Epley

Darin Erstad

Vince Ferragamo

Adrian Fiala

Mike Fultz

Gerry Gdowski

Turner Gill

Aaron Graham

Anne Hackbart

L. Dennis Hastert

Ryan Held

Jon Hesse

Suzanne Hince

Isaiah Hipp

Gene Huey

Dave Humm

Keith Jackson

Jeff Jamrog

Craig Johnson

Calvin Jones

Keith Jones

Mickey Joseph

Chad Kelsay

Larry Kramer

Mitch Krenk

Lee Kunz

Dennis LeBlanc

Keven Lightner

Pat Logsdon

Bruce Mathison

Charlie McBride

Jim McClurg

Jim McFarland

Steve McWhirter

Andy Means

Paul Meyers

Mike Minter

Malcolm Moran

Mark Moravec

Bobby Newcombe

Bob Newton

Herschel Nissenson

Danny Noonan

Mike Osborne

Nancy Osborne

Doak Ostergard

Stan Parker

John Parrella

Kent Pavelka

Bo Pelini

Harvey Perlman

Jason Peter

Terry Pettit

Jack Pierce

Jim Pillen

Chuck Pool

Jeff Quinn

Dave Rimington

Johnny Rodgers

Jim Rose

Steve Runty

Kelly Saalfeld

Rand Schleusener

Dan Schmidt

Jim Scott

Tom Shatel

Matt Shaw

Dal Shealy

Will Shields

Bryan Siebler

Jim Skow

Neil Smith

Bill Snyder

Brenden Stai

Anthony Steels

Ed Stewart

Eric Stokes

Barry Switzer

Jerry Tagge

Steve Taylor

Milt Tenopir

Broderick Thomas

Jeff Tomjack

Mike Tranmer

Matt Turman

Travis Turner

Pat Tyrance

Kris Van Norman

Henry Waechter

Jim Walden

Cartier Walker

Don Walton

Jim Wanek

Steve Warren

Jerry Weber

Doug Welniak

Tom Welter

Erik Wiegert

Jerry Wilks

Joel Wilks

Jamie Williams

Grant Wistrom

Randy York

Keith Zimmer

ABOUT THE AUTHORS

PAT WILLIAMS (ORLANDO, FLORIDA) – Pat Williams is the co-founder and senior vice president of the NBA's Orlando Magic. He is also a popular motivational speaker averaging over 150 appearances a year. Williams has spent 50 years in professional baseball and basketball as a player and executive. He served as general manager of the 1983 world champion Philadelphia 76ers and managed both the Chicago Bulls and Atlanta Hawks.

Williams is the author of over 75 books. He and his wife, Ruth, are the parents of 19 children, including 14 adopted from four nations. He and his family have been featured on major network shows such as *Good Morning America, The Today Show, Fox & Friends,* and *Mike and Mike* as well as in such diverse publications as *Sports Illustrated, Reader's Digest, Good Housekeeping, The Wall Street Journal,* and *Focus on the Family.*

MIKE BABCOCK (LINCOLN, NEBRASKA) – For 35 years Mike Babcock has written about Cornhusker athletics, beginning at the *Lincoln Journal and Star*, where he was a columnist and Nebraska beat writer. He also has written for *Huskers Illustrated* and is now the editor of *Hail Varsity*, a magazine dedicated to Husker athletics. Babcock has written and edited a dozen books, one on Nebraska basketball history, the others on Nebraska football. He and his wife Barb live in Lincoln.

Printed in the USA
CPSIA information can be obtained
at www.ICGtesting.com
JSHW012050140824
68134JS00035B/3368

9 781599 323794